Building Communication Partnerships With Parents

Melissa Marie Aronson, Ed.D.

Teacher Created Materials, Inc.

Cover Design by Darlene Spivak

Made in U.S.A.
ISBN 1-55734-846-4
Order Number TCM 846

Table of Contents

Introduction...i

Why Are School & Parent Partnerships Important?..................................1

What Does the Research Say?...7

Models of Home & School Partnerships...21

Ideas for Building Partnerships 29

In Conclusion..73

References..75

Introduction

"It takes a whole village to raise a child." The ancient African proverb has proven its wisdom over the ages and provides insight into a great deal of what can be improved in education today.

Building Communication Partnerships With Parents begins with a theoretical and philosophical framework as well as a review of research and current thinking about the need for and value of partnerships between home and school. Special needs of parents in our increasingly complex and diverse society are considered.

The majority of this book discusses specific strategies for building the communication partnership. Guidelines are suggested for publicity, accommodations, building a sense of partnership, and evaluating activities. Specific activities are identified and discussed with sample letters and flyers for adaptation to the readers' needs. The specific activities reviewed include:

- School-wide picnics and potlucks
- August open house
- Back-to-school night and open house
- Translations for non-English speaking parents
- Newsletters
- A call a day
- Report cards
- Parent and teacher conference techniques
- Interactive parent-teacher journals
- The parent center
- Welcome video
- Parent welcome and outreach
- Tips for success booklet
- Parent handbook
- Parent nights

Working together, educators and parents can greatly improve the opportunity for children to excel academically and socially. This book offers ways to begin the partnership.

Why Are School & Parent Partnerships Important?

Setting a Context

Visualize a school, your school, where:

◆ the children are excited about learning

◆ discipline problems are minimal

◆ the learning environment is structured so all children have an excellent opportunity to succeed

◆ students work on meaningful curriculum projects that extend beyond the school day to evenings and weekends where their parents work with them to succeed

◆ the parents support the school politically and with resources

◆ parents and community members provide tutoring to students in need

◆ parents bring their career, cultural, linguistic, and other skills to school to enrich the curriculum

Impossible? Perhaps not. Schools today are often lacking in material and human resources. Teachers are frequently frustrated by the

Visualize a school, your school, where the children are excited about learning.

perceived lack of support from the home, the community, and from taxpayers. Increasingly, schools are asked to accept more and more of the traditional child-raising responsibilities formerly taken on by the family and the community. Educators, including teachers and administrators, often feel they are alone in the overwhelming task of raising and educating children.

Conversely, parents today are concerned with the negative influences bombarding their children and greatly puzzled by the future that awaits their children. The schools are increasingly perceived as dangerous places troubled by overcrowding, lack of resources, and insufficient communication with the home. Parents often feel they are alone in the struggle to raise their children.

What If Educators Built Partnerships With Parents?

Many benefits can accrue from parent involvement in the schools through effective communication partnerships.

Many benefits can accrue from parent involvement in the schools through effective communication partnerships. Research evidence indicates parent involvement raises the academic achievement of students, improves the attitudes and performance of children in school, helps parents understand the work of schools, and builds school-community relationships in an ongoing, problem-preventing way (Rich, 1987).

The introduction to this book presented the ancient proverb "It takes a whole village to raise a child." The "village" of contemporary society is a complex and interdependent web comprised of the nuclear and extended family, school, neighbors, friends, community, churches, recreational opportunities, health providers, social service providers, business and industry, and many others. No longer is the "village" an extended family where everyone knows each other and has the luxury of trusting one another.

The complexities and size of modern society are coupled with economic pressures and time constraints on the family. The result is often a situation where we are interdependent on other members of our society that we simply do not know and, therefore, do not trust. The sense of "village" or community is lost. The specific causes of this loss of sense of community is the fodder of much discussion in the media and among people concerned with the lack of connectedness felt by many in modern society.

In many ways children have suffered most from the loss of community because they no longer have a cohesive group of people working together to raise them.

Working together as a "village" we can provide the best possible opportunities for children to succeed academically and socially. We can improve education by focusing on the relationship between the two primary stake-holders in the success of a child: the parents and the school.

Building Communication Partnerships With Parents is designed to help K–8 educators establish and improve two-way communication between the schools and the families. In order to set a context, let us look briefly at some definitions.

Building can be defined as the act or process of constructing. Building communication partnerships with parents is a thoughtful and deliberate act; it is not haphazard. It takes time, resources, a vision, and a great deal of work.

A home builder begins with a vision of the form and function of the home, develops blueprints, locates the resources, and then constructs a home in a deliberate and organized fashion. The result is a strong, beautiful, and functional home.

If, instead, a home builder does not construct a plan and just haphazardly nails together some boards that are lying around, the result is a shack that is drafty, structurally unsound, and only minimally functional as a temporary shelter.

And so it is with building communication partnerships with parents. The effective educator needs a vision of what type of communication partnership is desired. He or she must then develop a blueprint for action. Secondly, the educator should find the resources to bring the blueprint to fruition. Finally, the plan needs to be implemented in a deliberate and organized fashion. The result will be a communication partnership that will have broad benefits for children, teachers, parents, administrators, the school, and the community. Hastily drafted communication with parents may result in structurally unsound and only minimally functional communication that can cause more harm than good. Therefore, a solid communication partnership requires solid planning. A communication partnership can be built by one teacher with the parents of her or his students. Of course, like any major initiative, the communication partnership will be strongest if it is supported by the site administration and involves all the teachers.

Communication is the exchange of thoughts and messages by speech, signals, and writing. Communication implies two-way interaction with each party serving as both sender and receiver. In

Communication implies two-way interaction with each party serving as both sender and receiver.

3

building communication partnerships with parents, then, the communication channel involves both educators and parents sending out messages and receiving messages. Communication in this context is not comprised solely of one-way messages from the school to the parents.

Effective communication also involves honesty about the intent of the communication. Many of us have participated as members of advisory boards where we thought our advice would be taken seriously by those receiving our wisdom. How frustrating it is to discover that the findings of advisory committees are often only considered window dressing to meet some compliance requirements. Similarly, with communication between parents and the schools, it is important that the schools let the parents know the limit of the scope of communication. Do not involve parents in curriculum committees if their voices cannot be heard over existing requirements. Do not involve parents in discipline committees if the district or school already has an immutable discipline code in place. Insincere two-way communication can do more harm than good. Long-lasting partnerships, built on mutual respect, require effective two-way communication.

Partnerships are formal or informal contracts in which each partner agrees to furnish a part of the resources and labor for an enterprise and by which each shares in some proportion of the success or failure. Partnerships can be found in business, marriage, friendship, or in the schools. In this case the partners are the parents and school who provide the natural resources of a child and a curriculum. Both parents and the schools must become partners to actively provide material resources and care-giving resources to realize the success that comes from a well-educated child.

How Do We Begin?

The communication partnership with parents can be organized around three questions that appear on the surface to be rather simple but, in fact, can provide the philosophical structure for a deep analysis of many aspects of education. The three questions are:

◆ Who are the learners?

◆ What is worth teaching and learning?

◆ What is the most effective way to teach and learn?

Who are the learners? Teachers, through their education, training, and experience, can provide insight into learners as a group. A fourth grade teacher understands how fourth graders in general act and learn in formal settings. Parents, on the other hand, through their love and

Long-lasting partnerships, built on mutual respect, require effective two-way communication.

long-term association, provide insight into their specific child. The parents of the fourth grade student know how their child acts and learns in an informal setting. Together, the partnership of parents and teachers can provide deeper insights into "who are the learners" as they examine together general attributes and specific qualities. The child benefits from this combined understanding.

What is worth teaching and learning? Teachers can describe the formal school curriculum; parents can describe what their child likes to learn when left to her or his own devices. Together parents and teachers can share insights and resources to structure the curriculum to meet the needs and interests of each child. They can work together toward a common goal and a mutual understanding of "what is worth teaching and learning." Students interested in what they are learning are more involved, more successful, and better behaved.

What is the most effective way to teach and learn? Teachers can describe current methodologies used in the classroom and examine concepts such as learning styles and multiple intelligences. Teachers can also provide parents with ideas about how to support learning in the home. Parents can describe how their child learns best and provide a supportive learning environment at home. Together, parents and teachers can develop a cooperative plan to help each child learn in the most effective way.

Students interested in what they are learning are more involved, more successful, and better behaved.

Concluding Remarks

Building communication partnerships with parents can create a win-win-win situation. The schools win, the parents win, and most importantly, the children win.

The students win by becoming more successful in meaningful ways in schools. Research cited in the next chapter indicates that children more involved in the schools achieve academically and socially. This translates to increased education and leads eventually to increased earnings in their careers when they become adults. Many of our children-at-risk benefit enormously from an increased feeling of connectedness between themselves, their parents, and their schools.

Parents win as they lose their sense of isolation and see their children succeed. Public opinion polls and other research cited in the next chapter indicate that the more parents and the public in general know about schools, the more highly they rate them. Additionally, as schools build bridges for parents from a variety of cultural backgrounds, the parents lose their sense of isolation from the rest of the community and are seen as the resources they are.

Educators win as they work in an enriched environment with enthusiastic children who are encouraged at home. Many teachers express frustration over the perceived lack of interest by parents in their children's education. Building the partnership increases the involvement and interest of parents and, therefore, makes teaching a more rewarding endeavor for teachers.

School and parent partnerships can create a school where the children are excited about learning, discipline problems are decreased, parents support the school, tutoring is provided to students with special needs, and parents are resources on culture, language, and careers. All this will enable the learning environment to become structured so all children have better chances to succeed and can continue their learning beyond the school grounds and the school day.

What Does
the Research Say?

Introduction

Many scholars, researchers, government leaders, and philosophers have written in recent years about the relationship between parents and schools. This chapter provides a brief look at governmental and leadership recommendations, research from the Gallup Poll, on public attitudes about the schools relative to parent involvement research of what parents can do to assist their children to be more successful, and information about the changing nature of the family in terms of structure and diversity.

Readers wishing further information are referred to the bibliography and to *Strong Families, Strong Schools: Building Community Partnerships for Learning*, an excellent and concise document available through the U. S. Department of Education (1994). *Strong Families, Strong Schools* is available by calling 1-800-USA-LEARN.

Many scholars, researchers, government leaders, and philosophers have written in recent years about the relationship between parents and schools.

Governmental Recommendations

Goals 2000, the national education goals delineated in the Educate America Act (Public Law 103-227), identifies eight goals that have received bipartisan support and the endorsement of major organizations of parents, educators, and business. The goals, to be met by the year 2000, are as follows:

◆ 1. All children in America will start school ready to learn.

◆ 2. The high school graduation rate will increase to at least 90 percent.

◆ 3. All students will leave grades 4, 8, and 12 having demonstrated competency over challenging subject matter including English, mathematics, science, foreign languages, civics and government, economics, art, history, and geography. Every school in America will ensure that all students learn to use their minds well, so they may be prepared for responsible citizenship, further learning, and productive employment in our Nation's modern economy.

◆ 4. The Nation's teaching force will have access to programs for the continued improvement of their professional skills and the opportunity to acquire the knowledge and skills needed to instruct and prepare all American students for the next century.

◆ 5. United States students will be first in the world in mathematics and science achievement.

◆ 6. Every adult American will be literate and will possess the knowledge and skills necessary to compete in a global economy and exercise the rights and responsibilities of citizenship.

◆ 7. Every school in the United States will be free of drugs, violence, and the unauthorized presence of firearms and alcohol and will offer a disciplined environment conducive to learning.

◆ 8. Every school will promote partnerships that will increase parental involvement and participation in promoting the social, emotional, and academic growth of children (U. S. Department of Education, 1994).

Goals 2000 is an ambitious and noble agenda for the schools. It can be argued, however, that the goals are in the wrong order. If the eighth goal of promoting partnerships with parents was given first priority, the other goals would be easier to attain. Schools and parents working together in a partnership is a key element in the success of students.

Every school will promote partnerships that will increase parental involvement and participation in promoting the social, emotional, and academic growth of children.

With a solid partnership between schools and families, children are more likely to start school ready to learn (goal 1). Students who begin school successfully develop confidence in themselves as learners. That confidence forms a foundation for success throughout the school years and increases the chances that children will carry their success forward toward meeting the competency standards and eventual high school graduation (goals 2, 3, and 6).

High school graduation has important financial implications for the family and the individual. People who graduate from high school will earn, on average, $210,000 more during their lifetimes than people who do not graduate from high school. College graduates will earn almost $1,0000,000 more during their lifetimes than people who do not graduate from high school (U. S. Bureau of the Census, 1994). The wage-earning discrepancy between the well-educated and under-educated is increasing. Service sector careers are dividing into two distinct classes of well paid professionals and poorly paid hamburger flippers. "Work throughout the $6 trillion U.S. economy is skewing more sharply than ever along educational lines. We're getting the good jobs and the bad jobs, but the middle jobs we're losing" (Greenwald, 1994, p. 73).

High school graduation has important financial implications for society as a whole.

High school graduation has important financial implications for society as a whole. Through the 1990's one million students are expected to drop out of school each year, at an estimated cost of $240 billion in lost earnings and lost taxes over their lifetimes (Gilman, 1991). Parental partnerships with schools can go a long way toward helping students be successful in school, thus increasing the earning potential of individuals and helping the economic climate as a whole.

The Carnegie Council on Adolescent Development (1989) in *Turning Points: Preparing American Youth for the 21st Century* conducted an excellent analysis of the needs of these students. The needs of middle school students (grades 5 to 8) are not restricted to that age level, but rather have implications for earlier and later grades. The Carnegie Council identified eight recommendations:

◆ 1. Create small communities for learning where stable, close, mutually respectful relationships with adults and peers are considered fundamental for intellectual development and personal growth. The key elements of these communities are schools-within-schools or houses, students and teachers grouped together as teams, and small group advisories that ensure that every student is known well by at least one adult.

9

◆ 2. Teach a core academic program that results in students who are literate, including in the sciences, and who know how to think critically, lead a healthy life, behave ethically, and assume the responsibilities of citizenship in a pluralistic society. Youth service to promote values for citizenship is an essential part of the core academic program.

◆ 3. Ensure success for all students through elimination of tracking by achievement level and promotion of cooperative learning, flexibility in arranging instructional time, and adequate resources (time, space, equipment, and materials) for teachers.

◆ 4. Empower teachers and administrators to make decisions about the experiences of middle grade students through creative control by teachers over the instructional program linked to greater responsibilities for students' performance, governance committees that assist the principal in designing and coordinating school-wide programs, and autonomy and leadership within sub-schools or houses to create environments tailored to enhance the intellectual and emotional development of all youth.

◆ 5. Staff middle grade schools with teachers who are expert at teaching young adolescents and who have been specially prepared for assignment to the middle grades.

◆ 6. Improve academic performance through fostering the health and fitness of young adolescents by providing a health coordinator in every middle grade school, access to health care and counseling services, and a health-promoting school environment.

◆ 7. Reengage families in the education of young adolescents by giving families meaningful roles in school governance, communicating with families about the school program and students' progress, and offering families opportunities to support the learning process at home and at the school.

◆ 8. Connect schools with communities, which together share responsibility for each middle grade student's success, through identifying opportunities in the community, establishing partnerships and collaborations to ensure student's access to health and social services, and using community resources to enrich the instructional program and opportunities for constructive after school activities.

All eight of the Carnegie Council recommendations are worthy of consideration. Of most importance here for all grades is the seventh recommendation to "reengage families." Many of the suggestions

Youth service to promote values for citizenship is an essential part of the core academic program.

provided later in this book provide ways to improve communication with families about the school program, to involve parents in the academic and social progress of their children, and to support the learning process at home and at school.

Public Attitudes About Parental Involvement

For the last twenty-six years Phi Delta Kappa, in cooperation with the Gallup Poll, has conducted a national survey to measure the public's attitude toward the public schools. Since 1982 the poll has asked people to rate schools on a scale of A to F. A consistent finding over time is that the more people know about a school, the higher they rate it (Elam, Rose, & Gallup, 1994). Of the people with children in school, 70% gave the school an A or a B. If the school is in the community, but the respondent does not have a child in attendance, 44% gave the school an A or a B. On the other hand, general respondents gave the nation's schools considerably lower grades; only 22% award the nation's schools an A or a B.

When asked if the schools have improved, become worse, or stayed the same over the last five years, a similar trend appeared. Nationally, 16% reported the schools have improved, and a slight majority (51%) felt they had become worse. Compare that to attitudes of parents with children in the public schools; 36% thought the schools had improved, and only 15% thought they had become worse. The poll provides a great deal of other analyses and concludes:

> *What can one make of these responses? It seems likely that the general public has come to believe public education's critics regarding the state of the nation's schools, which have been blamed for everything from ignorance of geography to economic recession. Parents with children in school know better; a comfortable majority of them believe that the schools their children attend are improving* (Elam et al., 1994, p. 47).

The Gallup Poll (Elam et al.) listed educational quality and standards as the fifth priority in response to the question "What do you think are the biggest problems with which the public schools of this community must deal?" The most frequently mentioned concerns, in priority order were: (1) fighting, violence, and gangs (2) lack of discipline (3) lack of proper financial support and (4) drug abuse.

What do parents want from the schools? Research from a number of sources indicates that parents want the schools to do more than

Research from a number of sources indicates that parents want the schools to do more than just provide an academic education.

11

just provide an academic education. John Goodlad (1984) in his landmark book *A Place Called School* summed up his research on the above question to state:

In seeking to improve our schools, we may discover that some gains in standardized achievement test scores will not satisfy the full array of interests that parents and students have in their schools, interests that reach to the whole of life and extend well beyond academics (Goodlad, 1984, p. 75).

Other research on developing partnerships with parents cited by Stevenson (1992) has identified a series of nine priorities parents have for their children.

Parents want their children to be challenged academically and to achieve, but they want learning goals to be realistic.

◆ 1. When their child goes to school, parents want to know that he or she is safe, especially about things like the bus, changing classes, the cafeteria, and free time. They want to be assured that their youngsters will feel safe and be safe throughout the day.

◆ 2. Parents want their child to know at least one adult to approach when problems develop and have that adult know the child well enough to be of help with those problems.

◆ 3. Parents expect the school to see that constructive interpersonal relationships are emphasized.

◆ 4. Parents associate their children's happiness with the degree to which youngsters feel they belong to the total school program.

◆ 5. Parents want their youngsters to have enough successful experience each day to reinforce their good feelings about returning the next day.

◆ 6. Parents want their children to be challenged academically and to achieve, but they want learning goals to be realistic.

◆ 7. Parents want teachers to keep their children informed about their progress, and they seek opportunities to work in concert on problems. They especially want to know their role in homework.

◆ 8. Parents want to feel welcomed at the school, known by their names, and invited for more than just parent conferences.

◆ 9. Parents want schools to help them learn more about what youngsters are like at this stage in their development, provide seminars, support groups, and access to resources and professional organizations.

In summary, surveys consistently indicate that parents rate schools more positively if they are involved in the school. Parents also indicate they want to be involved in their child's education. Here is more good news! Not only are parents favorable toward the school, many of them are willing to volunteer in the schools. The 24th annual poll indicated that 54% of men and 64% of women were willing to work as unpaid volunteers in their schools. This and other data leads the authors of the poll to conclude "these findings suggest that school authorities may have failed to take full advantage of a rich resource in troubled financial times" (Elam, Rose, & Gallup, 1992, p. 31).

Are parents, in fact, too interested in the schools? Do they want to take over the management? Goodlad notes that while polls show that parents would like a greater say in the schools, they do not want to take over the running of the schools. Parents want open communication that keeps them informed about the progress and welfare of their child.

What Can Parents Do to Help?

The document *Strong Families, Strong Schools*, published by the U.S. Department of Education in late 1994, reviews thirty years of research documenting the role of the family in the learning of children. The evidence cited overwhelmingly supports the importance of the family as a predictor of the school success of a child. Parental participation improves student learning regardless of the age of the child, the socio-economic status of the family, or the educational level of the parents. The study documented a number of ways that parents can have a positive influence on their children's education.

◆ 1. *The first and most obvious parental action is to control absenteeism.* The child who is not in school is not learning the school curriculum. The research on time-on-task points to one very simple but powerful conclusion: the more time a child is on task, the more the child learns. Also, the child who is absent from school may be getting involved in at-risk behaviors.

◆ 2. *Providing a variety of reading materials in the home, and reading themselves, is a powerful model for parents to provide.* The literature can be wide and varied and include magazines, as well as books. It can be purchased, borrowed from the library, or acquired at a garage sale. Research evidence indicates that students who read for pleasure have higher academic achievement (Mullis, Campbell, & Farstrup, 1993) and better reading comprehension (Lee & Croninger, 1994).

Providing a variety of reading materials in the home, and reading themselves, is a powerful model for parents to provide.

13

◆ 3. *Monitor television watching.* The average eighth grader spends less than 6 hours per week on homework and more than 21 hours watching television (Gilman, 1991). While some television watching is a normal part of our society and apparently not harmful, academic achievement has been found to drop sharply for children who watch more than 10 hours per week (U. S. Department of Education, 1994). The quality of the television is also significant. Parents can make television watching a positive influence through careful selection of programs and family discussions after viewing a show.

◆ 4. *Read aloud to children.* Reading aloud has been thoroughly documented to have a significant effect on children from early ages. As every parent or grandparent who has read to children knows, they begin to enjoy the sound of reading, to associate pictures with the story, and to connect the written and spoken word at early ages. Sadly, only half of parents with children under the age of 9 report they read to them every day (U. S. Department of Education, 1994).

◆ 5. *Establish a daily family routine.* As difficult as it is in our overly busy society, established routines help children know when it is time for homework and bed. Parents who include a discussion of the school day in the daily routine can help their children a great deal. Probing questions about the day can help the child reflect and keep the parents aware of progress. One sample question is, "Can you tell me something you learned in school today?" followed by a conversation about the learning.

◆ 6. *Provide a schedule and place for homework.* Children need a comfortable, well lit place with as few distractions as possible to do their homework. It is also helpful if the time for homework is predictable. Parents should also monitor homework to make sure it is done completely and accurately and communicate with the teacher if the child is having undue difficulties. Research has shown that students with low aptitude scores who spend a significant amount of time on homework get as good grades as children with more aptitude who do not do homework. (U. S. Department of Education, 1994).

◆ 7. *Monitor out-of-school activities.* Many of the children who become involved in at-risk behaviors suffer from lack of adult supervision.

◆ 8. *Take time for parent/child conversations.* These conversations can lead to higher achievement (U. S. Department of Education, 1994). These conversations are appreciated by youngsters. Seventy-two percent of children between the ages of 10 and 13 said they would like to talk to their parents more about school work (National Commission on Children, 1991). These conversations are a good time for parents and children to learn about each other.

◆ 9. *Communicate positive values and character traits such as respect, hard work, and responsibility.* What parents say and do is still the most important influence on children's lives.

◆ 10. *Hold high expectations for achievement.* The expectations should be realistic, but challenging.

Research is clear on the effect of parental actions on student achievement. The factors indicated above are all important independent factors. The influence may be even stronger as the factors combine symbiotically. For example, three factors alone—student absenteeism, lack of reading materials in the home, and excessive television watching—account for nearly ninety percent of the differences in standardized math scores of eighth graders.

> **Research is clear on the effect of parental actions on student achievement.**

Other sources (California State Department of Education, 1987) cite another way parents can help their children, and that is to stay involved with the school as children get older. Parental involvement declines dramatically as students move through the grades. Many parents are involved with primary age youngsters, but fewer are actively involved by the time children reach the middle school and high school years. A study at Johns Hopkins discovered that only a third (34 percent) of the parents who regularly visited their child's elementary school, regularly visited the middle school when the children were enrolled there.

Hodding Carter stated the responsibilities of parents well: "There are only two lasting bequests we can hope to give our children. One of these is roots; the other, wings" (Peter, 1977, p. 103).

The Changing Nature of the Family

But wait! The family structure has changed. Families are rarely the traditional "Ozzie and Harriet" families of the 1950's anymore. How can parents be expected to provide positive influences? How can effective partnerships be established between parents and the schools? What is a "family"?

Many families in the 1990's do not resemble the idealized family of the 1950's. It is beyond the scope of this book to describe all the changes that are occurring in the structure we call "family" or to discuss in depth the effects of those changes. Let us focus briefly on a few characteristics of today's family that may effect the types of partnerships that can be established between home and school: career demands; single parents and non-traditional family structures; educational level; and cultural, ethnic, and linguistic diversity.

Career Demands

The nuclear family is generally defined as two parents and their children. In the 1990's both parents are likely to be working in order to meet the economic needs and wants of the family. Working parents face serious constraints on their time and energy. Forty percent of employed parents say they do not have enough time to spend with their children (Finney, 1993). Many children are left to their own devices before or after school and may get inadequate supervision, including lack of supervision of homework. In fact, in one study one-third of all eighth graders report that no adult relative has ever talked with them about their schoolwork (Gilman, 1991).

The school needs to be flexible about when parents are available, how much time they have, and how that time is used.

What are the implications for attempting to build communication partnerships with parents when both work? The school needs to be flexible about when parents are available, how much time they have, and how that time is used. One possible solution is for events to be organized around evening hours and weekends. For example, parent conference days can be held on a nonteaching day with the conference times from 2 P. M. until 8 P. M. One high school recently tried this schedule. Concern had been expressed by the faculty that very few parents came to conferences, and it was difficult for teachers and parents to communicate. The faculty decided not to send report cards home, but rather to schedule an open conference time where parents could come to the school, pick up the report cards, and meet with the teachers. The day was designated a nonteaching day. The teachers arrived on campus shortly after lunch and conferences were held from 2 P. M. until 8 P. M. Estimates are that 2,500 parents came for the conferences (C. Roberds, personal communication, November 14, 1994).

Parents who are busy with career demands need to have their time used wisely. Programs should be designed to be efficient and targeted to the purpose of the event. If it is necessary, for example, to read the minutes of prior meetings or to have a financial report, set aside an adequate block of time for those details before or after the meeting. Establish a "time certain" to begin and end the business portion of the meeting and the content portion of the meeting.

Single Parents and Nontraditional Families

Approximately half of all marriages in the United States end in divorce; that statistic has been relatively stable for many years (Swap,

1993, p. 14). Divorce has many consequences for a child. The child's time and loyalty may be divided between the custodial parent and the noncustodial parent. Children often feel they are somehow responsible for the divorce and may need intensive counseling and support. Children may find themselves having to provide emotional support for the newly divorced parent. Economic conditions are frequently worse after divorce. There may be a remarriage and a blended family with stepparents and half siblings and stepbrothers and sisters with all the attendant adjustments.

Increasing numbers of children are born to women who are not married, some by choice and some not by choice. In some cases children are born to, or raised by, same sex couples. While these situations are more widely accepted now than in the past, these children and their parents may still have special needs.

The number of teenage parents has risen in the last few years; indeed, the United States leads the developed nations in the per capita number of teenage pregnancies (U. S. Bureau of the Census, 1994). Teenage parents are often not prepared to adequately take on the responsibilities of parenting. Much has been written about the problems of children raising children and their lack of preparation for the role of parenting.

Some children live in an extended family situation with parents, grandparents, aunts, uncles, and cousins under one roof.

Some children live in an extended family situation with parents, grandparents, aunts, uncles, and cousins under one roof. These children may have needs quite different from the children of the two-career families. Instead of too much time alone, these children may have difficulty finding a quiet time and place to study. Instead of too little supervision, these children may have too many bosses, often providing conflicting messages.

Some children live in foster homes in short-term or long-term situations. Foster parents have parenting thrust upon them, albeit voluntarily. Foster home environments have special needs, such as development of communication skills.

Sadly, more and more families are homeless. Some programs are developing to assist parents and children who are homeless so that the children can get adequate educations. The Transitional Learning Center in Stockton, California, is an excellent model of an effective program; indeed, the program has been the recipient of many national awards. For information, contact the Transitional Learning Center at (209) 467-0703 or (209) 667-3367.

Educational Level of Parents

A common tendency is to judge education based on one's own experience. Many people, when talking about education, will recount their own personal experiences, including their likes and dislikes, their successes and failures. And so it is with parents. Some had excellent educational experiences in their schooling and fine support from their own parents. Some had very poor educational experiences and little or no support at home. Most fall somewhere in between. As schools attempt to develop partnerships with parents, it is important to remember that these "ghosts of schooling past" exist. Sometimes the first task in developing a partnership is to exorcise those negative memories.

By all accounts, the United States is increasingly becoming a majority of minorities.

Some parents are well equipped academically to help their children with school work. But alas, some parents are academically deficient. For example, one in six Americans is functionally illiterate and reads at lower than the 6th grade level (Gilman, 1991). In order for parents to help children with schooling, the schools may first have to help the parents with literacy and numeracy.

Cultural, Ethnic, and Linguistic Diversity

By all accounts, the United States is increasingly becoming a majority of minorities.

> *The United States, more that any other county on Earth, is a nation of immigrants. Since the formation of the U.S., we have accepted 60 million legal immigrants, more than all the other nations combined. We are currently experiencing one of the three largest influxes of immigrants in our history. Earlier migrations tended to be largely from one geographic area, easing the process of integration. The current wave of immigration is more global, bringing a wider range of diversity* (Aronson, 1994, pp. 7–8).

Immigrants and refugees may have had very little experience with formal education themselves as children. They may find the school a strange and threatening environment. The curriculum may be largely incomprehensible for the unschooled parent. The schools' expectations about student behavior may be in violation of the families' traditions relative to student behavior. As an example, placing male and female students together in the same class may produce culture shock for some parents and actually lead to forced early marriages of middle school children (Holtgate, 1994).

On the other hand, some immigrant parents are highly educated. Their school experience may be quite different from the U. S. experience in that they attended school where the teachers were highly respected and students were held to high account for their achievement. These parents may be appalled at what they perceive to be the loose discipline and low expectations of the American elementary school classroom.

The schools need to provide adequate services for immigrant children, their families, and their teachers. Programs for immigrant children include bilingual education, sheltered instruction, and SDAIE programs (Specially Designed Academic Instruction in English).

Nonimmigrant children need an educational emphasis on multicultural and global education to develop their appreciation of the diversity brought by their immigrant peers.

Teachers need education in multicultural education and language acquisition.

Immigrant parents may need assimilation programs to help them learn English and develop life skills to become successful in the United States. An excellent model program is the BRIDGE in Modesto, California, that provides services to Cambodian refugees. The BRIDGE can be reached at (209) 571-8430.

Teachers need education in multicultural education and language acquisition. In California most teacher credential programs offer a CLAD (Culture, Language, and Academic Development) credential or certificate. The CLAD provides education on theory and practice for working with students who are English language learners. For more information, contact the California Commission on Teacher Credentialing (916) 445-7254.

Concluding Remarks

The eighth recommendation of Goals 2000 encourages schools to promote partnerships that will increase parental involvement and participation in promoting the social, emotional, and academic growth of children.

The research cited in this chapter provides a positive connection between some vital factors:

- ◆ Parents have more positive attitudes about schools if they are involved at the school.
- ◆ Parents often express willingness to participate in the schools.
- ◆ Parental participation improves student learning.

19

The research on building partnerships has to be applied to the contemporary family. The concept of family has changed tremendously over the last few years. The nuclear family is often comprised of two wage earners. Many families are headed by single parents or are blends of two or more nuclear families. Increased immigration has provided a cultural, ethnic, and linguistic resource waiting to be tapped by the schools for its richness. All of this variety can be a strength in developing partnerships between home and school. Composite research on individual families indicates family income or education levels are not as important to the academic success of a student as what the family does to support the education of the child (U. S. Department of Education, 1994), and that support can come from every family.

Many schools have been able to build partnerships using a variety of methods and models. The next chapter provides an overview of different types of communication models between home and school. The fourth chapter provides a number of ideas for building home and school partnerships.

Models of Home & School Partnerships

Introduction

Home and school relationships take many forms across the nation and have been classified into three categories: the patriarchal model, the school-to-home communication model, and the partnership model. Some examples of each model may be found at any given school.

The patriarchal model uses traditional top-down management.

The Patriarchal Model

The patriarchal model uses traditional top-down management. It has three major attributes (Swap, 1993):

(1) parents delegate to the school the responsibility of educating their children

(2) parents hold the school accountable for the results

(3) the schools accept this delegation of authority and take on increasing responsibility for raising children

The patriarchal model of communication, to the extent that it exists, is largely top-down within the school and one-way from the school to the parents. The patriarchal school is characterized by the principal who is the "boss" and the teachers who are the "workers." Directions are given to teachers from the principal.

The top-down approach of the patriarchal school continues to the relationship between the school and the parents. The public and parents assume that that schools are relatively autonomous institutions. Feedback to parents about the progress of their children is generally limited to one-way communication including report cards, back-to-school night, and open house.

Report cards provide a letter grade assessment of the student's progress in various academic disciplines and an indication of social development (e.g., "follows directions well," "gets along well with others"). The report card may provide a small area for teacher comments. Provision for parent response is generally limited to a signature and a small area for comments.

School events that inform parents about the academic program are limited in scope. The most common forms are back-to-school night and open house. Both events are largely teacher-centered. Back-to-school night is generally held at the beginning of the school year. The teacher usually gives a presentation about the goals for the year, an overview of the curriculum, a description of any innovative instructional methods, and a statement about expected behavior. Parents can ask general questions but cannot discuss their own child with the teacher.

Open house is frequently scheduled toward the end of the school year. Parents visit the rooms of their children and have a chance to observe some selected activities completed by the class as a whole. Often portfolios are available for each child so parents can look at their work. Like back-to-school night, no time is available for individual parent-teacher conferences.

With the patriarchal model the schools take on increasing responsibility for raising children in four areas:

(1) academic, including intellectual skills and knowledge

(2) personal, emphasizing personal responsibility and creative endeavors

(3) social and civic, focusing on socialization and citizenship

(4) vocational, preparing students for the world of work

Parents, teachers, and students generally rate all four areas as very important roles for the schools, with some variation based on the grade of the children. Vocational preparation is rated lowest of the four in elementary school but increases in importance as a child moves through the grades.

When asked to rate each of the four areas in terms of relative importance, most elementary parents (57.6%) rate academic goals highest. Personal goals are ranked second by nearly a quarter (24.5%) of the respondents. Social goals and vocational goals are rated as most important by a minority of parents (9.3% and 8.6% respectively) (Goodlad, 1984).

The schools are faced with increasing demands in academic, social, personal, and vocational goals. Schools are expected to address the increase of knowledge in the information age, the need for computer literacy, social responsibility in a time of increasing violence, and personal education in an age of sexually transmitted diseases (especially AIDS). Additionally, the schools are expected to provide health services, a growing number of social services, lunch, and increasingly often, breakfast. These demands are intruding on an already full curriculum and school day. The result is that teachers, especially elementary teachers, often feel overwhelmed by the accumulating responsibilities of the patriarchal school.

> **The schools are faced with increasing demands in academic, social, personal, and vocational goals.**

Unless schools undergo a significant shift in organization and move away from the patriarchal model, the responsibilities faced by the schools will become increasingly impossible to address adequately.

The School-to-Home Communication Model

This model assumes a somewhat increased partnership. Within the school the site administration involves the teachers in discussions and committees within a prescribed range of authority. Initiatives for change generally originate with the administration.

Communication between the home and school operates with more openness than the patriarchal model and incorporates three assumptions (Swap, 1993):

(1) a child's academic achievement is assisted with consistent expectations and values between school and home

(2) educators should identify practices and values in the home and community that contribute to school success

(3) parents have a responsibility to reinforce the importance of education through cooperation with the school

Again, communication is largely from school to home, with the school telling the parents what they should do and with parents complying to varying degrees.

The expectations for the child's academic achievement are established by the school. Communication takes the form of open house and back-to-school night and is enhanced through newsletters from the principal or teacher that go home to the parents.

The school assumes that the family and community have the same vision of the goals and the importance of education that are espoused by the schools. The vision of the schools tends to be very much middle class in orientation. There is a largely assumed agreement that a major purpose of schools is to prepare students for college. Curriculum is designed and defended as being necessary for "next year." "You need to be able to read to be successful in second grade." "You need to know your multiplication tables for fourth grade." This rationale is continued through the grades until it is stated as, "You need this for college." Even the college is not immune. How many of us have heard, "You need this for graduate school?" Insufficient attention is given to how students can use their newly found knowledge and skills right away.

The school-to-home communication model incorporates a form of parent-teacher conferences. Conferences are generally initiated by the teacher, either to discuss a problem with the student or in conjunction with handing out the report cards. The agenda of the conference is usually established by the teacher. The teacher essentially tells the parent about the progress of the student or the deficits of the student. Together the parent and teacher agree about what needs to be done by the home to support the efforts of the school. It is important to note in this description that the communication line here is largely from the school to the parent. The parent is expected to comply with the school's directions.

In some cases parents are not able to meet the expectations established by the school. If enough parents are deemed to need help meeting these expectations by the school, parenting education classes may be formed to help parents be better parents. The teachers, principal, and other members of the school team are generally responsible for establishing the curriculum of the parenting education classes. The overriding goal is to help parents learn better how to help their children with school work, thereby assisting the schools with their mission. The parent center, described in the chapter "Ideas for Building Partnerships" provides some suggestions.

> **Together the parent and teacher agree about what needs to be done by the home to support the efforts of the school.**

The school-to-home model is an improvement over the patriarchal model because it increases the number of channels of communication and offers some elements of two-way conversation. But the school is still not fully utilizing an available and willing resource base: the parents.

The Partnership Model

The final model is based on a true partnership. In the schools the authority moves toward "site-based management" where the teachers have a substantial role in the direction, leadership, and administration of the school. The principal works with the teachers in a collegial relationship and there is an underlying philosophy that the school ecosystem can be improved with the positive contributions of all.

The partnership model as it applies to relationships between home and school has four underlying assumptions (Swap, 1993):

(1) communication is two-way between the home and the school

(2) home and school are interdependent in providing for a successful educational experience for the child

(3) a common vision exists about the desired outcomes of the partnership

(4) the partners agree that the communication model is constantly evolving and improving

In the partnership model the communication is two-way between the school and the home. The school personnel talk to and listen to the parents and the parents talk to and listen to the teachers and administrators. Two-way communication is essential in building a meaningful relationship, whether in a friendship, marriage, parenting, business, or between home and school. Together they can address the questions: Who is the learner, and what is worth teaching? The remainder of this chapter establishes a framework for developing the partnership model of communication. The chapter "Ideas for Building Partnerships" provides suggestions for practical implementation ideas.

The partnership model recognizes that home and school are interdependent in helping children reach their full potential. The ancient African adage, "It takes a whole village to raise a child" says it so well. The parents offer some resources to the partnership and the school offers others. Without both sets of resources, the child suffers.

> In the partnership model the communication is two-way between the school and the home.

Both home and school need a common vision about the desired outcome of the partnership. From the very beginning it is important to establish the parameters of the relationship. The school needs to be forthright in describing the limitations of the partnership, such as regulations from the district, state, or federal government. Parents need to be honest about their limitations, such as time and economic constraints. Once the limitations are openly acknowledged, the partners have the opportunity to build a plan that will work.

Nothing is perfect from the beginning. All ideas evolve over time as needs change and experience is accumulated. Parents and the school need to agree that the partnership plan will also change and improve over time.

Both home and school need a common vision about the desired outcome of the partnership.

Are there specific steps that can be used to develop a partnership and improve it over time? One framework is provided in *The 7 Habits of Highly Effective People* by Stephen Covey (1989). In the book he identifies seven steps to increased personal effectiveness. Those steps with adaptations for developing home-school partnerships are:

(1) *Be proactive.* Deciding to establish a school and parent partnership is a proactive first step. That proactive first step can be initiated by the principal, teacher(s), or parent(s).

(2) *Begin with the end in mind.* Start with a planning meeting between parents and the school staff, including administrators, teachers, counselors, and other support staff. Some suggestions for the planning process follow later in this chapter.

(3) *Put first things first.* Work together to establish a priority list of activities to build the partnership.

(4) *Think win-win.* Better yet, think win-win-win. In an effective home and school partnership there are three winners: the parents, the school, and most importantly, the children.

(5) *Seek first to understand...then to be understood.* The patriarchal communication model and the school-to-home communication model are both deficient in this essential quality; both seek primarily to be understood first. In the partnership model both the parents and the school staff seek first to understand the other and then to make themselves understood.

(6) *Synergize.* The combined resources of the home and the school can work together to provide for the best possible upbringing for children. In synergy the whole is greater than the sum of the parts, and so it is with an effective partnership.

(7) *Sharpen the saw.* Be sure to include plans for ongoing assessment of the partnership to improve and refine the goals and activities.

"Ideas for Building Communication Partnerships," a later chapter, provides some concrete ideas for building communication partnerships with parents. Because the partnership involves two-way communication, it is vital for the school personnel and the parents to meet together to discuss the establishment of the partnership. The parent and teacher team is encouraged to accept some ideas, reject others, modify suggestions, and add new ideas.

This planning meeting establishes a climate for the communication partnership. It is important that the meeting be carefully planned to convey an authentic interest in a partnership. Some recommendations and questions to consider in planning the meeting are listed below.

Be sure to include plans for ongoing assessment of the partnership to improve and refine the goals and activities.

- ◆ The meeting is open to all parents, teachers, administrators, counselors, and support staff. Should other interested members of the community be invited also?

- ◆ How will child care be provided? Child care is vital to the success of the meeting.

- ◆ For what languages are translators needed?

- ◆ What time or times are convenient for both parents and school personnel?

- ◆ Where can the meeting be held that is a comfortable, non-threatening, and informal setting?

- ◆ How can the meeting area be structured for equitable give and take between parents and school personnel? Circles work well.

- ◆ What kind of refreshments should be available?

- ◆ Name tags are a useful tool to encourage communication. Do you have enough?

- ◆ Should the meeting begin with some sort of mixer to encourage people to get to know each other?

- ◆ Does the agenda include:
  - setting the context with a definition of a partnership?

  - brainstorming the ways parents and schools can work together to help children?

- reaching a consensus about a vision for building communication partnerships?

- developing a blueprint for action?

- identifying resources to bring the plan to fruition?

- agreeing on an implementation plan?

- developing a method to assess progress and improve the partnership?

Concluding Remarks

The partnership model recognizes the essential role of the parents in the effective education of their children.

This chapter has reviewed three basic models of home-school partnership: the patriarchal model, the school-to-home model, and the partnership model. The attributes of each model have been discussed. The patriarchal and school-to-home models both put the vast majority of the responsibility on the schools. The partnership model recognizes the essential role of the parents in the effective education of their children. With the partnership model the schools are no longer seen as a separate piece of the life of a child. Rather, the schools are viewed as part of the whole ecosystem of school, community, and home, which is vital to the successful development of children.

Ideas for
Building Partnerships

Introduction

The beginning of this book established a rationale for the importance of building communication partnerships with parents. First we examined why school and parent partnerships are important. Next, we reviewed relevant research. Following the research we looked at three models of home school communication and concluded with suggested guidelines for a planning meeting to establish communication partnerships between parents and the school. This chapter provides a potpourri of ideas that can be incorporated into home and school partnerships. The chapter begins with general guidelines and then provides a variety of ideas.

This chapter provides a potpourri of ideas that can be incorporated into home and school partnerships.

General Guidelines

Sometimes even the best planned event fails because of some oversight that turned a potential success into a disaster. Ask experienced teachers, principals, or parents and they can probably tell stories about events where the flyers were not sent out in a timely manner, or not sent out at all. Or, that meeting rooms were locked and no one could locate the janitor. The marquee in front of the school announcing the event had a misspelled word. The needed A-V equipment was not available, did not work, or the light bulb had burned out. No outlet was available in the room for a coffee pot. The speaker did not have adequate directions to the school or did not realize how long it took to get to the school from where he or she lived. Needed supplies were missing. No day-care was provided and the entire meeting was disrupted by crying babies and bored kids. No one was available to clean up. The list of disasters goes on and on. Some are humorous in the telling long after the event; few were a source of laughter at the time.

Careful planning is needed in advance of each event and planning meeting to make sure that people will attend and all will go as anticipated. Let us examine four planning strategies: (1) publicity (2) accommodations (3) building a sense of partnership and (4) evaluating the activity.

Careful planning is needed in advance of each event and planning meeting to make sure that people will attend and all will go as anticipated.

Publicity Strategies

Ideas for publicizing your event include the following ideas:

◆ Announce the event well in advance. An annual calendar of events can be distributed at the beginning of the school year. Additional announcements should be made a month in advance with a reminder a week ahead of the actual event.

◆ Make the invitation personal. Invitations can be made by the children, the teacher, the parents, the administration, or some combination. Proofread the announcement for spelling and grammar errors and to make sure it addresses the who, what, when, where, why, and how questions. Provide written translations as appropriate. Write the announcement at a level appropriate for the parents.

◆ Establish a telephone tree for each classroom to communicate quickly. The teacher, principal, or any of the parents should have access to the telephone tree. One way to organize a telephone tree is to have parents as the base. Whoever wishes to initiate the communication calls the "base" three parents. Those three call three more each; now nine people have been called. Those nine in turn call three each; now twenty-seven have been reached. The numbers can be modified, depending on the number of calls to be made. Out of respect for everyone's time constraints, no one person should have to call more than five people. Selected people at the end of the tree should be asked to call the initiator to confirm that the message went out. If you have parents who do not speak English, make sure they are contacted by another parent fluent in their language.

◆ Use word of mouth to supplement written invitations. This is particularly effective to involve parents who have not participated in past activities or who are new to the school. Active parents can call inactive parents and perhaps even offer to provide a ride. This can increase participation and possibly initiate a friendship, thus helping to end the isolation many parents feel.

◆ Door prizes can be awarded to encourage participation. Alternately, a prize can be given to the class with the highest attendance level.

◆ This is a partnership. Parents, teachers, and administrators have a responsibility for communication.

Accommodations

Accommodations can make attending the meeting easier and much more pleasurable, thereby increasing future participation. Some strategies include:

◆ Schedule events at times convenient for both parents and teachers. No single time works for everyone, so a variety of times increases the chance for everyone to participate. Events can be held during the school day, in the late afternoon, in the evening, or on the weekend. It may be possible, for example, for parent conference day to be a nonteaching day and to hold conferences from 2 P. M. until 8 P. M.

◆ Provide child care. Many free and inexpensive resources can be identified with a little ingenuity. The local high school or college may have a child development class; students could get course credit for assisting with child care at your event. Retired teachers or others experienced with large groups of children may be available. Perhaps the children can be incorporated into the event itself.

◆ Hold the meeting in a comfortable and nonthreatening environment that is conducive to a sense of partnership. Classrooms can be very threatening to some parents as they are flooded with less-than-positive memories of their own school experiences. Arrange seating to establish a sense of collaboration; circles work well. Provide everyone (teachers, principal, parents, etc.) with name tags to encourage communication.

◆ Make sure that parking is convenient and the parking area is well lighted for evening events. If necessary, provide a security guard for the parking area and escorts for parents walking alone.

Accommodations can make attending the meeting easier and much more pleasurable, thereby increasing future participation.

◆ Have welcome signs and directions to the event. Provide the signs in the languages of the families at your school.

◆ This is a partnership. Administrators, parents, and teachers have a responsibility for providing appropriate accommodations.

Building a Sense of Partnership

Building the partnership between teachers and parents is, of course, the purpose of the event or activity. Some strategies to build the partnership include the following:

◆ Remember that a partnership means all members of the team are actively involved in the planning and implementation of the event. Make sure parents, teachers, and administrators work together on all aspects of the activity.

◆ Include short ice-breaker mixer activities into events to encourage parents, teachers, and administrators to interact with one another.

◆ Provide seating arrangements that mix teachers and parents together. Make sure the administrative and support staff also commingle.

◆ Involve parents and school staff together in planning activities, preparing publicity, organizing the events, and providing refreshments.

Evaluating the Activity

Reflecting upon and evaluating the activity provide a basis for continued development of the quality of the partnership program. Some ideas follow.

◆ Keep track of the number of people who attend each function and their roles in the school by using a sign-in sheet.

◆ Ask participants to evaluate each session. Keep the evaluation process simple with a rating form, suggestions for further activities, and a place to indicate activities in which they would like to become involved. At the end of the chapter is a "Samples" section that begins with a suggested format for an event evaluation (pages 51–52) for the mythical Stepping Stone School.

◆ Maintain records of the activities, when they occurred, and the ratings.

◆ Develop a data base of suggested activities from the evaluation sheets.

> Building the partnership between teachers and parents is, of course, the purpose of the event or activity.

- Develop a data base of suggested activities from the evaluation sheets.
- Develop a data base of parents, teachers, and other school staff who have indicated an interest in becoming involved and their choices of activities.
- This is a partnership. Administrators, parents, and teachers share the responsibility for evaluation.

Specific Strategies

Now let us look at some specific strategies designed to develop partnerships. In this section a number of ideas are presented. Examples for many are included in the "Samples" section at the end of the chapter.

School-Wide Picnics or Potlucks

The goal of school-wide picnics should be to encourage informal socializing between the school personnel and parents. They can be a true partnership activity. School-wide picnics or potlucks should be held on a regular basis (e.g., monthly or quarterly). The picnics should be structured so that school personnel (teachers, administrators, support staff) and parents are encouraged to mix and mingle. In fact, structured getting-to-know-you activities need to be included to encourage such socializing.

The picnic should include activities for the children that will not require supervision by the parents or the teachers. Yard duty supervisors and/or high school students are assigned responsibility for the children.

Simultaneously, some enjoyable mixer activities need to be held for the parents and school staff. The goal of the activities is for everyone to get to know each other and to break down barriers.

Some schools have had success by including a cooking contest in the picnic/potluck activities. The contest can be broad based or focus on ethnic foods or foods produced in the region. See the example of the Citrus Harvest Festival on page 53.

The responsibilities for organizing and cleanup should be shared equitably between parents and the school. During the activity itself neither parents nor school personnel should have any responsibilities that will get in the way of communication; instead hire needed help. All too often at school functions the school personnel are too busy with responsibilities to be able to visit with parents and the benefit of the event is lost.

> The goal of school-wide picnics should be to encourage informal socializing between the school personnel and parents.

During the picnic it is not appropriate for parents and teachers to have one-on-one meetings about specific children. Rather, teachers have appointment books either with them or at a designated location where parents can make appointments for in-depth parent-teacher conferences.

August Open House

The purpose of the August open house is to communicate with parents about the upcoming school year prior to the beginning of school. In year-round schools this should be done prior to the beginning of each new grade. In order to involve as many parents as possible, hold the open house on a nonteaching day over an extended time so that parents can attend, no matter what their work schedules.

The open house is a time for the teacher to discuss school policies, review the school calendar, and preview the curriculum.

Mail the invitations to the parents approximately two weeks prior to the open house, with a reminder notice in the local newspaper. Since some of the parents will be unfamiliar with the school, include a school map. The invitation should include an agenda. Remember that some of your parents do not read English; be sure to provide translations as appropriate. An example invitation follows on pages 54–55.

During the open house have the teacher and parents introduce themselves and spend some time getting to know each other. Parents should be invited to participate in the home and school partnership and surveyed about their interests.

The open house is a time for the teacher to discuss school policies, review the school calendar, and preview the curriculum. Parents are encouraged to ask questions. The teacher may involve parents in a mini-lesson that uses some of the curriculum and methodology (e.g., cooperative learning) that is incorporated during the school year.

Individual appointments should be made between the teacher and the parents for the parents to provide insight into the child's learning needs and preferences. At these conferences the teacher should question the parent about health problems, the child's academic progress to date, insights into how the child learns best, indications of multiple intelligences, and the child's social development. Together the parents and the teacher develop some guidelines about how the home and school can work together best to assure the child has a successful year. Both the parents and the teacher need to make honest commitments about ways they intend to help the child.

Back-to-School Night and Open House

These activities are designed to bring together teachers, parents, administrators, and students during the school year to review the progress of each student.

Send invitations to parents at least two weeks in advance of the event, with a follow-up reminder a few days before. The children can prepare the invitations for their parents. A sample open house invitation pattern follows on page 56.

During back-to-school night and open house, use some of the time in an unstructured format for parents to review the progress of their child. Each student should have a portfolio of work demonstrating progress and an interactive journal. The journal can be free flowing in its content or can contain prompts such as "What I learned today," "In our special project I learned that...," "I learn best when...," "Next weekend I would like to learn more about...," and "Over vacation I would like to learn about..."

The portfolio is a means of authentic assessment and includes significant examples of a student's work. The portfolio should demonstrate student achievement in a variety of content areas while using a range of cognitive skills. Traditionally, some of the portfolio entries are selected by the teacher, some by the student. However, in all cases the teacher and student will discuss together the contents of the portfolio. The more mature the student, the more input he or she should have in the contents of the portfolio.

The student may also prepare an interactive journal which contains a letter to the parents from the child about school; the parents respond with a letter to the child. The letter from the parents could include some comments on the portfolio. Stickers, stamps, and other visual additions could be available for parents to add to the journal entry as positive reinforcement for the child's efforts.

Structure some of the time during back-to-school night and open house as an opportunity for teachers to share some information with parents and answer questions. The presentation might include:

◆ Selected information about the teacher (family, education, hobbies)

◆ Overview of the year in terms of curriculum

◆ Discussion of instructional methods (cooperative learning, individualized instruction)

The portfolio is a means of authentic assessment and includes significant examples of a student's work.

- New ideas you are trying this year
- Daily schedule
- General procedures about absences, homework, etc.
- Discipline philosophy and expectations
- Ways parents can assist in the classroom, at special events (e.g., field trips), and at home
- Above all, ways to communicate and work together as partners for the success of each child
- Questions parents may have

The structured time during open house and back-to-school night could be used for children to teach a mini-lesson to the parents about something they have learned. Alternately, the children might perform a simple production such as readers' theatre.

If possible, offer simultaneous translation throughout all events.

Because of time constraints and confidentiality, it is not appropriate for parents and teachers to discuss individual students. Instead, teachers must have appointment books either with them or at a designated location where parents can make appointments for in-depth parent-teacher conferences. In the spirit of the partnership, parents need to be actively encouraged to make appointments. Further suggestions for successful open house events follow on page 57.

Translations

We are increasingly a nation of recent immigrants, and many classrooms have students whose parents are not English speakers. Therefore, it is useful to translate any and all invitations, handouts, signs, and directions into parents' native languages. If possible, offer simultaneous translation throughout all events. Presenters should have training in sheltered language techniques to make the presentation more comprehensible to parents who are still learning English. Translation is an area where bilingual parents can be an excellent resource. When translations are useds for relatively short written communication, provide the translation on the same sheet with the English message. The languages can be either side by side or one above the other. In long letters it may not be feasible to provide the message in different languages together. In that case, be sure to include the same graphics and maintain print and paper quality to communicate a sense of equity.

Providing written communication in English and other languages helps parents realize the linguistic diversity of students at the school. It also provides an opportunity for English reading parents to become more familiar with other written languages and for non-English reading parents to improve their English reading skills.

The multilingual communication to parents can also become a teachable moment in the classroom as the teacher and students discuss language diversity. Students fluent in other languages can teach the teacher and their classmates some of the language, both verbal and written. The students learning the second language can then teach their parents.

An example of a bilingual flyer in English and Spanish entitled "Stepping Stone School Reminder" is on page 58. It is followed by an example of a trilingual flyer in English, Spanish, and Hmong entitled "Holiday" on page 59.

Newsletters and Other Written Communication

Newsletters written by teachers and administrators are primarily for the purpose of school-to-home communication. Newsletters can be published on a regular basis (e.g., every other week or monthly) or can be used for specific communication needs.

Let us look at some general hints for effective newsletters and then review some examples. Hints for effective newsletters include the following:

◆ Use the same color, quality, and size paper for all of your newsletters so parents become familiar with your communication "set." This is an effective strategy for magazines (e.g., *National Geographic*) and can be effective for you as work-weary parents sort through a stack of papers brought home by their children.

◆ Carefully check the newsletter for accurate information.

◆ Ask someone not associated with the school to proof the newsletter to make sure it does not include inaccurate assumptions about what someone will know about the school.

◆ Use the spell and grammar checker.

◆ Talk to the parents, not at them. Remember that the goal of your newsletter is to communicate and build partnerships.

◆ Consider using graphics in the newsletter that the children can color for their parents.

◆ Provide translations of the newsletter as appropriate. Parent volunteers can be quite useful for this important task.

Remember that the goal of your newsletter is to communicate and build partnerships.

◆ Conduct a readability analysis of the newsletter to make sure it is at a level appropriate for your parents. To set a context for adult reading levels in general, most newspapers are written at about the sixth grade reading level. Unless you are working with a highly educated parent population, sixth grade level is probably the maximum level you want. Many readability scales (e.g., the Fry) measure the number of syllables and sentences in a passage. A passage can be made simpler by using less complex words and shorter sentences. Conversely, a passage can be made more complex by using longer words and sentences.

◆ Have the children address the newsletter to their parents.

◆ With young or unreliable students, let the parents know where you will put the newsletter (e.g., in a side pocket of a backpack) and consistently use that place.

◆ Include a section that is written by the children in the newsletter.

◆ A question/answer format is effective for some types of information.

Conduct a readability analysis of the newsletter to make sure it is at a level appropriate for your parents.

Newsletters to communicate specific information include introductory letters to parents at the beginning of the school year. Two examples follow on pages 60 and 61. The first example is designed to help build partnerships with parents. The second sentence "A good learning experience is built on a cooperative effort among parent, child, and teacher," sets the partnership tone immediately. This example goes on to establish high expectations for students, to ask for volunteers while providing a rationale ("The more specialized help students receive in class, the more they will learn"), and to ask for information from the parents about the student. It concludes with an invitation for parents to initiate communication.

The second letter has a different thrust of letting parents know about the teacher and the teacher's philosophy of education. It also concludes with an invitation for parents to contact the school.

Another type of communication that may be useful early in the school year is to provide parents with a list and explanation of supplies students will need for successfully completing their homework. See the sample letter entitled "Supplies for Home Study" on page 62.

Sometimes the communication to parents requires that they respond to the teacher. For example, many teachers want to know that parents understand what the expectations are for student behavior in the classroom and have a list of established classroom rules. See the sample letter entitled "Classroom Rules" on page 63 as an example. Note the response portion of the communication at the bottom for parents to return to the teacher. If it is important for parents to respond, so be sure to maintain a checklist to record when students return the response forms. Specifically ask the students for the forms. Send reminders after two days, and follow up with phone calls after one week.

As noted earlier, parents generally express a willingness to help in their child's school. In order to get parent volunteers, it is important to make sure the activity the parents are involved in is useful, is something the parents want to do, and is at times convenient for the parents. The example letter entitled "Volunteer Help Needed" on page 64 is a good start; if possible, consider extending the days and hours for active volunteer time.

As noted earlier, parents generally express a willingness to help in their child's school.

Supply budgets for schools are often inadequate. Where can teachers find resources for science labs and other activities? Many supplies are available at home and can be found in the ubiquitous "junk drawer." See the example of a letter sent home to request materials entitled "Parent Letter for Homemade Rocks" on page 65.

At some point early in the year it is useful to send parents some ideas on how to help their child. These tips can be reinforced throughout the year as "fillers" for other communication pieces. A newsletter example entitled "Ways to Help Your Child" follows on page 65.

The newsletter can be structured in an attractive way by using seasonal "stationery." See the example of "September News" on page 67.

Let us now look at a newsletter from a principal to the parents entitled "Principal's Pen" on pages 68–70. As you read through the example, look for the following:

◆ "Thank you" messages to specific parents by name

◆ Information about upcoming events and dates

◆ Report card information and parent responsibility

◆ An invitation to join the School Site Council, the partnership program at that school

◆ News tidbits about the school and faculty

◆ Tips to parents to help their students with school

◆ A positive, inclusive tone that talks with parents, not at them

A Call a Day

Phone calls from the school are often assumed by parents to be initiated because of a medical emergency or because a child is in trouble. What would happen if phone calls were made because a child was doing well? In fact, this can be an excellent strategy to keep communication lines open between teachers and parents. Best of all, it only takes about 5 minutes a day. Let us look at a sample phone call and some partnership building characteristics.

> "Hello, Ms. Smith. This is Ms. Tammy Teacher from Stepping Stone School."
>
> "Oh no! Is Sally O.K.?"
>
> "She's fine."
>
> "Then what kind of trouble is she in?"
>
> "No trouble at all! I'm just calling to tell you how well she is doing in learning her multiplication tables. She knows all her number facts up through multiplying by fives. This is a big improvement for her! She has been working hard to make so much improvement."
>
> "Well, I have been testing her at home; maybe it's working!"
>
> "It certainly seems to be. Let us look at some ways we can work together to help her learn the rest of her multiplication facts."

Remember this strategy for building partnerships is "a call a day."

The conversation continues covering the ways Sally learns best, what the parent and teacher have noticed about what works for Sally, what does not work for her, and how they can help her further. Typically, the conversation will end something like this:

> "Well, Ms. Teacher, I have to say I was worried when you called! I'm not used to getting positive phone calls from the school. I really appreciate your calling me with good news! Please let me know if there is anything I can do to help with the classroom."

Remember this strategy for building partnerships is "a call a day." One call takes about 5 minutes and can be easily worked into the school day. If a teacher calls one parent a day, that is five a week; by the end of six or seven weeks, the parents of all the students will have been called once. The cycle can then repeat, and over the course of a year each parent will be called five or six times. The pattern for a call a day is to select one student a day and call home. The call focuses on the successes of the student, with specific commendations for improved behavior or achievement. The call should then proceed to a partnership-building conversation as the parent and teacher explore ways to help the student become even more successful.

The teacher should keep a record of which students have been called and the dates to provide for equitable contact with the parents of all the students. It may be useful for both parents and teachers to keep brief notes on the student success identified and the parent and teacher plans to help the student continue to grow.

Because the phone call is positive in nature, it provides reinforcement for all concerned. The parents are reinforced with positive contact from the school. The teacher gets to focus on the success of a student and to receive thanks from a parent. The child arrives home to find out the teacher called with praise. Once students find out that the teacher calls a parent a day, it is not unusual for children to ask the teacher to call their parents.

This relatively simple, 5 minute a day commitment can do a great deal to change the nature of home and school communication and build parental and community support for the teacher and the school.

Report Cards

In theory, report cards are an effective and important way for schools to communicate to parents. But reality and theory can be quite different. How can report cards be designed to increase the sense of partnership between home and school?

Many different report card formats are available for consideration. Some attributes to look for include:

- ◆ an analysis of academic development in different content areas
- ◆ an analysis of cognitive development in terms of different skills
- ◆ an analysis in terms of the student's strengths relative to learning style and multiple intelligences
- ◆ a report on the student's social development, including ethical behavior, conflict resolution skills, and response to stress
- ◆ a space for the teacher to write a positive note
- ◆ a space for the teacher to describe specific goals for the student to work on over the next few weeks

Once students find out that the teacher calls a parent a day, it is not unusual for children to ask the teacher to call their parents.

◆ suggestions by the teacher for ways the parent can help the child at home

◆ an emphasis on solutions rather than labels

◆ a place for the parent to respond in a meaningful way to the teacher

◆ establishment of a sense of partnership among the student, parent, and teacher

Some schools are beginning to incorporate a report card conference into the grading process. These events are developed to bring parents to the school to meet individually with teachers about the progress of their child. Each conference is kept to a short schedule of approximately 15 minutes. Should there be a need for a longer conference, one is scheduled.

Report card conferences seem to be most effective if they are scheduled on a nonteaching day with a beginning time of about 2 P. M. and an ending time of about 8 P. M. A potluck dinner can be incorporated into the day as a social event. Running the day on a 2 P. M.–8 P. M. schedule allows teachers to meet with working parents.

For those parents unable to attend the report card conference, an alternate appointment is established, or the report card is sent home by mail and a follow-up phone conference is held.

Report cards, used carefully, can be an effective way to build communication bridges.

Parent-Teacher Conferences

The goal of parent-teacher conferences is to reach a mutual agreement between parents and teachers on ways to help children become more successful students. Conferences can either be in person or by phone. They can be scheduled because the student has demonstrated particular success or need, or because the conference is a school-wide scheduled event at report card time. For ideas about phone conferences that focus on success of the student, see the call-a-day suggestion earlier in this chapter.

Too often parent-teacher conferences are dreaded by both the teacher and the parent. Building a sense of partnership can eliminate the mutual uneasiness and result in a successful event that helps the child grow to the next level of achievement.

Let us look at some points to consider in conducting a parent-teacher conference, a way for both parties to prepare for the conference, and suggestions for the training of parents and teachers for conferences.

There are a number of points to consider that can help make a parent-teacher conference more successful. Those ideas apply to both the teacher and the parents and include:

- ◆ Agree at the beginning on the purpose of the conference.
- ◆ Take a few minutes to get to know each other. Ask the parents to share a bit about their own school experiences. This may give the teacher insights into the parental expectations for the school and of their child.
- ◆ Start the conference with positive statements about the child from both the parents and the teacher.
- ◆ Have a portfolio of the child's work available for review.
- ◆ Consider sending the portfolio home in advance of the conference so the parents can prepare for the conference.
- ◆ Have thorough documentation of the child's progress, including the gradebook and attendance records. Parents can bring samples of the child's work from home.
- ◆ Find areas where the teacher and parents agree.
- ◆ Make specific plans for change and progress, with both the parents and the teacher assuming specific responsibilities.
- ◆ Practice active listening where both parents and teachers work to understand each other's perspective. Both have important contributions to make to the success of the student.
- ◆ Treat all conferences as confidential.
- ◆ Keep other children out of the conversation. Do not compare this student with siblings or other students in the class.
- ◆ Be truthful but tactful. Unkind remarks are not needed and may cause defensiveness.
- ◆ Be cognizant of cultural differences which may affect communication.
- ◆ Involve a translator if necessary.
- ◆ Review together the unique characteristics of the child, including social and educational development, formal and informal learning preferences, and multiple intelligences.
- ◆ If appropriate, invite the child to join the conference.

There are a number of points to consider that can help make a parent-teacher conference more successful.

◆ Schedule the conference at a time convenient to both the parents and the teacher.

◆ Hold the conference in a comfortable setting.

◆ Sit side by side or in a way to demonstrate a partnership. The teacher should avoid the authority message that comes with sitting behind a desk.

◆ Speak English, not "educationese."

◆ Both parents and teacher should write out an agreement about the action to be taken. This could be done on NCR paper with both parties keeping a copy.

◆ Check for understanding to make sure communication is clear.

◆ Make definite and specific plans for follow-up.

The teacher should avoid the authority message that comes with sitting behind a desk.

Often it is useful for the teacher to send a preconference letter to the parents to establish a mutual agenda so both parents and teacher can prepare for the conference. An example "Preconference Letter" is provided on page 71.

If the teacher wants to establish an equitable partnership, the preconference letter could be reversed to come from the parents to the teacher. A request for conference form can be in the class newsletter.

It is useful to call to confirm the conference in advance. This is especially true if you are not sure of the language skills of the parent and want to establish whether you will need a translator.

Many parents and teachers report having inadequate training in how to conduct parent-teacher conferences. The parent center (see page 46) can include in its agenda training sessions for parents on effective conference skills. The session could include reviewing the ideas listed above plus training on active listening and assertive communication as opposed to passive or aggressive communication.

Teachers also need training in effective conference skills. Alas, it is a skill only rarely taught in preservice programs and in-service workshops. Such training can be highly effective, however. Recently, a group of student teachers took part in a training session on parent conference skills, including the ideas listed above. They then scheduled conferences with the parents of the children in their classes. With the parents' permission, the sessions were taped. The student teachers then listened to the audio tapes and evaluated themselves. This was their first experience with a parent-teacher conference. Their self-analyses follow on the next page.

I thought it went very well. I began and ended on a positive note. I was able to get the grandparent actively involved in the conversation. We had a very enlightening talk which lasted about 30 minutes. I learned a great deal about Tara and the grandmother learned some about Tara's school....I was very nervous....I also felt like I didn't talk enough. I spoke for maybe 5 minutes of the entire conversation. I should have been a little more prepared. I could have scripted out what I wanted to say. All in all I was pleased with the conference. It was definitely something I can chalk up to a learning experience. Next time I will be much better prepared (K. Coughran, personal communication, November 9, 1994).

The parent had experienced many negative conferences in person and preferred a phone conference. We spoke for 25-30 minutes and both of us felt comfortable. We both focused on the student's positive attributes and the conference took on the feeling of "together we will prevail"....it was a genuine sense of togetherness and we reaffirmed the lines of communication opened at the beginning of the semester. The entire conference was positive; even those characteristics that were highlighted as contributing to the student's poor performance...were mutually agreed upon and spoken of in terms of activities to help student gain confidence and improve. Another plus was that we both received feedback. Parent was interested in student's performance and volunteered student's perception of instruction and the student teacher. She intimated that she is pleased with the (student teacher) program. Question: have you ever considered getting assessment of student teachers from the parents? (S. Cardoza, personal communication, November 9, 1994).

....I went over an outline of the unit that Amanda was working on. I talked about the book we read, why we read it, and how Amanda enjoyed it. I explained that Amanda wrote in a journal on a daily basis, what she wrote, and why she wrote in it. I talked about...the fairy tale Amanda was writing. Amanda's mom was surprised that her daughter enjoyed writing fairy tales. She learned something new about her daughter.... Her mom was very pleased that I had positive things to say. I almost got the impression that she doesn't hear positive things from Amanda's teachers very often. ...This was a positive learning experience for me (C. Carlsen, personal communication, November 9, 1994).

The entire conference was positive, even those characteristics that were highlighted as contributing to the student's poor performance.

The parent-teacher conference should end with a written commitment by both parties about how to help the child succeed even more. For older children, the children might also be asked to make a commitment in writing about what they will do to ensure their own future success.

Interactive Parent-Teacher Journals

Many teachers have discovered the benefits of interactive teacher-student journals where the students and teachers communicate back and forth about the student's progress. The interactive parent-teacher journal is a similar concept that provides a chance for parents and teachers to write back and forth to each other on a weekly basis regarding the progress of the individual student. This can be an excellent follow-up to a parent conference.

Like student journals, the writing can be freeflowing or could incorporate prompts such as "Janey has demonstrated conflict resolution skills by...," "Jim learns best when he...," "A goal I have for Jose is..." Prompts can be rather limiting to the conversation but can be useful to initiate communication when necessary.

The Parent Center

If a true home-school partnership is going to flourish, parents need a place to meet on their own turf where they can establish a sense of belonging and equality in the school setting. The parent center provides a place for parents to meet, to develop programs, to do their support work, and to provide workshops for other parents.

The parent center may be a classroom not needed for instruction or a separate building designed just for parents. Finding the facility can be a challenge, but one the parents may take on as a goal. A portable classroom could be purchased with local donations. If a community center or library is located close to the school, it could be used.

The center should be scheduled to be open to accommodate parent needs; therefore, ideally it is open during the school day, in the evening, and on Saturdays. Keeping the parent center open should not be a burden on the school staff; rather, parents from the partnership team can be given the key and can keep the center open and maintained. If the center is part of the library or community center, access arrangements should be made through those agencies.

The center should include a business area with resources for an office: a computer or typewriter, copy machine, resource materials, graphics supplies, and so on.

The parents involved at the center can develop and present workshops for other parents on a variety of topics. The model is parents teaching parents. Teachers and other school staff are used only as resources as necessary. Some possible topics for workshops include:

- ◆ tutoring tips for parents
- ◆ how to help your child study
- ◆ understanding the curriculum
- ◆ resource and curriculum materials
- ◆ instructional innovations
- ◆ peer pressures and your child
- ◆ characteristics of successful parent-teacher conferences

If appropriate, the center could also provide literacy, numeracy, and life skills education for parents. It could also serve as a center for social and medical services to be provided to school families.

The costs for supporting the building can come from the school district, from parent/school fundraising, from grants, or from corporate and individual contributions. If the center has multiple uses for social and medical services, the costs can be shared among a number of service agencies.

Because it is a parent center, the parents should have prime responsibility for the center, including care and maintenance. Of course the parents need to be advised of current laws about appropriate behavior on the school grounds (e.g., laws about smoking, etc.).

Welcome Video

We are increasingly becoming a nation of people who learn by video. Why not take advantage of this trend? Each teacher could make a brief video (about 10 minutes) to welcome the students and parents to the school. The video might include a walk through of the campus, a shot of a school map, a tour of the classroom, portions of a lesson in action, a welcome to the parents, and an invitation to become involved in the parent-school partnership. Copies of the video should be available to send home whenever a new student enrolls in the school. A copy could also be sent home to parents who are reluctant or unable to participate in home-school partnership activities. Use parents to provide a narrative translation, if appropriate.

Each teacher could make a brief video (about 10 minutes) to welcome the students and parents to the school.

Parent Welcome and Outreach Teams

Parents often feel alone. The parent welcome and outreach teams are designed to help parents help other parents overcome feelings of isolation by providing friendship and involvement in school related activities. The teams welcome new families into the school, orient them to the community, show them the parent center, and invite them to join the home-school partnership.

Parents and teachers alike understand that each child in a classroom has an effect on the achievement and development of every other child in the classroom. Therefore, it is important that the parents of all the children be brought into the home-school partnership as much as possible. In order to achieve the broad base of effective support, the parent teams also provide outreach to parents who are inactive in supporting their children's education or who are in periods of personal crisis.

Parents and teachers alike understand that each child in a classroom has an effect on the achievement and development of every other child in the classroom.

"Tips for School Success" Booklet

The "Tips" booklet should be designed by the home-school partnership team. Rather than the school telling the parents what to do with their children to ensure school success, this booklet should emphasize parents communicating to other parents with some ideas about school success. The booklet should be designed and written by the parents, with the administration providing editing and checking for content accuracy. Clerical support should be offered by the school to the parents. If a parent center is established, the production of the booklet can occur in the center.

The booklet should provide tips to parents about how to support the education of their children by providing a quiet place to work, reviewing homework, and reading aloud to their children. It should provide information about the homework hotline. Additionally, the booklet may provide insight into how to contact the school, including the names and office phone numbers of administrators, counselors, school nurse, office staff, bus drivers, and other important school personnel. Other information items and tips are provided as deemed important by the parent writers. Like all communication between the home and school, provide translations as necessary. Bilingual parents can be an excellent resource.

Parent Handbook

The parent handbook should be designed by a team comprised of parents, teachers, counselors, and administrators. Parent involvement is important to ensure that the handbook is written for the parent audience and addresses their needs and perspectives.

The parent handbook includes information on the home-school partnership, including the goals of the partnership and how to contact the active leadership. It also includes the school goals and mission statement, a staff roster, the school calendar, the student handbook, discipline policy, and other important information. Like the "Tips for School Success Booklet" described above, the parents take a major lead in determining the content and doing the writing. Again, provide translations as appropriate, with bilingual parents serving as the translators.

Parents' Night

Some of the more innovative curriculum reforms (e.g., Family Math and Family Science) include parents in structured activities with the children. The activity provides the children, parents, and teachers with a chance to interact on problem solving activities related to the curriculum. The parents and children are encouraged to work together to build a project or solve a problem. To add extra excitement to the activity, families may compete against other families for the fastest, prettiest, and strongest product.

Should you decide to sponsor a parents' night, make sure to involve parents in the planning process.

Should you decide to sponsor a parents' night, be sure to involve parents in the planning process. A key to success is to make sure the parents have the knowledge base to be successful in the activity.

An example of an entry form for family teams for a family science night is located on page 72. The event may begin in the late afternoon with kite making and flying where families work together to make the kites. Following a light supper, the family competition begins with family teams competing against other families to make inventions out of used materials like milk cartons, aluminum foil, craft sticks, and the like. The activities from the Science Olympiad can serve as good starter ideas.

Family nights can focus, certainly, on more than science and math. A creative teacher can develop any number of different types of activities. Another family night activity to consider is a book fair. In order to conduct a book fair, have the parent-teacher partnership team contact local publishers, bookstores, and/or office supply merchants. Very often they are willing to bring their wares to a school for a book fair. In exchange for being able to sell merchandise, the merchants make a contribution of cash or books for the school library. Everybody wins: the library gets more books and students and their parents purchase books to read at home. Incorporate into the program a short presentation on the importance of parents reading to their children.

Samples

This section includes samples of ideas presented earlier in the chapter. The samples represent good ideas gleaned from a number of sources. The samples include:

◆ Event Evaluation (pages 51–52)

◆ Citrus Harvest Festival (page 53)

◆ Invitation for Open House (pages 54–55)

◆ Sample Open House Invitation (page 56)

◆ Suggestions for Successful Open House Events (page 57)

◆ Back-to-School Reminder (bilingual) (page 58)

◆ Holiday Letter (trilingual) (page 59)

◆ Introductory Letter to Parents #1 (page 60)

◆ Introductory Letter to Parents #2 (page 61)

◆ Supplies for Home Study (page 62)

◆ Classroom Rules (page 63)

◆ Volunteer Help Needed (page 64)

◆ Parent Letter for Homemade Rocks (page 65)

◆ Ways to Help Your Child (page 66)

◆ September News (page 67)

◆ Principal's Pen (pages 68–70)

◆ Preconference Letter (page 71)

◆ Family Science Night (page 72)

This section includes samples of ideas presented earlier in the chapter.

Event Evaluation
for
Stepping Stone School

Thank you for attending our (name of event).

Stepping Stone School has established a partnership program between the school and the parents of our children. We are always looking for ways to improve the partnership and make it more effective. It would be very helpful to us if you would fill out this two page evaluation sheet. Please do not put your name on this page; it is to be anonymous. The second page asks for your specific interests; therefore we need your name. Thank you for your assistance.

Did you enjoy the event? (circle one)

      Very much   It was O.K.   Not at all

What other Stepping Stone Partnership Programs have you attended within the last year? (Provide a checklist of activities over the last 12 months.)

How did you hear about the program?
      _____ from the school newsletter
      _____ from a personal invitation my child brought home
      _____ from a phone call from another parent

Did you meet other parents from your child's class?   Yes   No

Were you able to talk with your child's teacher(s) about (name of event)?
      Yes   No

Did you want to schedule an appointment for a conference with the teacher to discuss your child's progress?   Yes   No

If yes, were you able to schedule a conference?   Yes   No

Describe one thing you learned at (name of event):

Event Evaluation
for
Stepping Stone School *(cont.)*

Page 1 of our our evaluation is anonymous. However, on this page we ask that you provide your name so we can contact you for follow-up.

Name: _____

Child's name: _____

Child's teacher: _____

What are some other events you would like to see the Stepping Stone Home-School Partnership address?

In what ways are you interested in getting involved in the Stepping Stone School Partnership?

When is the best time to contact you? _____

What is your phone number? _____

Thank your for your interest in the Stepping Stone School Partnership. We will be in touch!

Stepping Stone Citrus Harvest Festival
Potluck and Recipe Contest
Saturday, (Month, Day, Year)
Entry Application
for
Best Use of Citrus Fruits in Food Contest

Name: _____

Address: _____

Zip: _____ Phone: _____

Dish to be judged: _____

Join us again this year for our Citrus Harvest Festival Food Contest and School Potluck. The event will occur in the multipurpose room at Stepping Stone School on (date) with judging from 12 noon to 1:30 P. M. Bring your dish to be judged to the multipurpose room by 11:30 A. M.

The winning recipes will be added to our Citrus Recipe Cookbook. Each year we add recipes, and each year the cookbook gets better! Our latest cookbook is available for purchase for $X.

Even if you do not want to enter the contest, please join us for our potluck which will begin at 11:30 A. M. Please bring one dish for the potluck and table service for your family. In addition to the recipe judging, we will have enjoyable mixer activities for children and adults.

Entry forms for the contest can be sent to school with your child, taken to the school office, or left at Smith's Super Market.

Stepping Stone School
Invitation to Parents
for
August Open House

August 10, (year)

Dear Parents:

We are looking forward to working with you and your son/daughter at Stepping Stone School.

Here at Stepping Stone School we have an active partnership program that includes parents, teachers, and administrators. We hope you will join us! The Partnership developed the program for this year's August Open House.

The Open House is for the parents of all children who will be enrolled at Stepping Stone. Children are invited to attend also; we have exciting recreational activities planned for them in the multipurpose room. For your convenience the program will repeat three times between 2 P. M and 8:15 P. M. Please attend at the time most convenient to you.

We have three events planned for you on (date) as well as appointment schedules for a follow-up, one-on-one meeting between parents and the teacher. The events are as follows:

1. Welcome to the school by the Stepping Stone Partnership Team. At this welcome you will be given a copy of the parent handbook with bus schedules, the school calendar, a staff roster, school map, discipline policy, school procedures, school emergency numbers, and information about the Stepping Stone School Partnership. This is a good chance to let us know how you would like to be involved in the Partnership. The welcome will be held in the school library. Translations will be available in (specify languages and make sure the written invitation is also in those languages). Please attend one of the three sessions at the following times:

2:00–2:30   4:00–4:30   6:30–7:00

Continued on the next page

2. Visit to your child's room to meet the teacher and participate in an interesting lesson. These sessions will be held in each teacher's room. Please attend one of the three sessions at the following times:

2:45–3:45   4:45–5:45   7:15–8:15

3. A potluck dinner for parents, children, teachers, and administrators. If you wish to participate, please bring your place settings and two dishes (main course, salad, potatoes/rice/pasta, vegetable, or dessert). The potluck will be held outside, weather permitting. Otherwise, we will meet in the cafeteria.

5:45–6:30

We want to make sure to arrange for one-on-one meetings between parents and teachers to discuss each child and for parents to provide insights for the teachers. Each teacher has an appointment book by the classroom door in which you can sign up for a meeting to take place sometime during the first two weeks of school.

For your convenience, a school map is below. We hope to see you on the (date)!

Sincerely,

Penny Principal   Paul Parent

(insert school map here)

Sample Open House Invitation

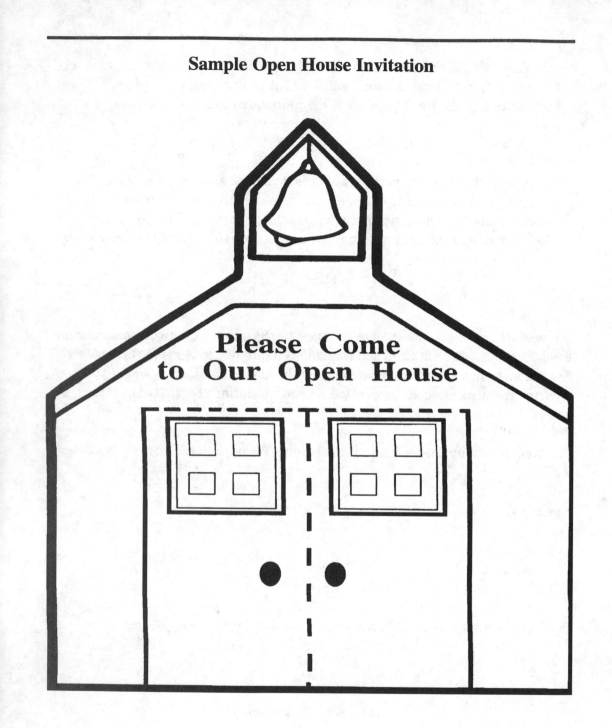

Please Come
to Our Open House

Suggestions for Successful Open House Events

There are things you can do to make an Open House celebration more successful and enjoyable for both you and your students and parents. Open House is not a night for personal conferences on student progress. Sometimes parents ask questions of that nature and will need to be reminded that this is not the night for conferences. Explain that you would be glad to schedule a time when you can talk with them on the telephone or in person. The following is a list of some of the things that may help you to have a successful Open House.

- Have the students make personal invitations for their parents.

- Post a variety of different kinds of student work around the room. Avoid using work that has grades on it, as parents will then compare.

- Label different work areas in the classroom as well as class projects that might be on display (like murals that were developed as part of studying a particular piece of literature, period of history, etc.).

- Have students make a room guide brochure to use with their guests the day of the event. This way you can be sure that everyone sees what you want them to see.

- Have students practice touring each other around the room, explaining and pointing out things of interest using their room guide brochure, so they will be ready to give guests the tour.

- If the time is right, use the Open House event as the culminating event for a thematic unit. Students might want to serve refreshments, do science experiments, act out parts of history, or whatever fits their unit.

- If possible, plan for students to have something to take home to share with their parents (art folder, writing collection, completed project).

- Enjoy the Open House yourself!

Reprinted from TCM149 Year–Round Teacher Tips, *Teacher Created Materials, 1991*

Stepping Stone School
Back-to-School Reminder

(bilingual example)

Dear Parents,

This is to remind you of the Back-to-School Night Program being held tonight, (date), at 7:00 P. M. We will be introducing our staff for the 1995–96 school year. As we did last year, we will have refreshments available.

Parents of track D students are to meet in the cafeteria. We look forward to meeting you tonight.

Sincerely,

Penny Perfect
Principal

****

Estimados padres:

Esto es para recordarles del Programa de Back to School Night (Noche de regreso a la escuela) que se llevara a cabo, esta noche 27 de agosto a las 7:00 P. M. Estaremos presentando a nuestro profesorado para el ano escolar de 1995-1996.

Los padres de estudiantes de sesion D en la cafeteria. Esperamos conocerlo/a esta noche.

Sinceramente,

Penny Perfect
Directora

58

Stepping Stone School District
Holiday Letter
(trilingual letter)

Dear Parents: October 10, (year)

All Stepping Stone School District schools will be closed Monday, October 15, in observance of school base coordinator program day.

We hope you will enjoy this time with your children, and we we look forward to having them back in school on Tuesday, October 16, when classes will be in session as usual.

Sincerely,

Susan Smith
District Superintendent
****

Txog ib tsoom niam-txiv   Hnub 10 lub 10 hli, (year)

Hnub 15 lub 10 hli, no nyob rau txhuya lub tsev kawmntawv hauv zos Stepping Stone so tsis kawm vim muaj (a day the staff receive training).

Peb vam tias nej yuav tau nrog nej cov menyuam nyob ua ke. Neo ntsoov rov xa lawv tuaj kawm hnub 16 raws lub sij hawm qub.

Noj qub nyob zoo,

Susan Smith
District Superintendent
****

Querido padres,   Octubre 10

Todo Stepping Stone escuelas de distrito de escuela estar cerrar lunes, octubre 15 en observancia de dia de programa de coordinador de base de escuela.

Esperamos te gozar de este tiempo con sus ninos, y esperamos tenerlos estar de vuelta en escula sobre martes, octubre 16 cuando clses estaran en sesion como usual.

Sinceramente,

Susan Smith
superintendente de distrito

Introductory Letter to Parents #1

Dear Parents,

I am pleased to take this opportunity to meet you and welcome your child to my class. A good learning experience is built on a cooperative effort among parent, child, and teacher. My expectations for conduct and standards for academic growth are high. With your participation in and out of the classroom, we can look forward to a productive, creative, and enjoyable year together.

In the past I have had many parents volunteer their time in the classroom. I encourage this because it provides opportunity for more children to receive one-on-one attention.

If you are interested in volunteering, please let me know. This can be on a weekly, bi-weekly, or occasional basis. The more specialized help students receive in class, the more they will learn.

I am excited about this new year. I hope we can work together to make it one of growth, discovery, and significance for your child.

You can help by giving me any information that will help me understand your child better. Some things I am interested in include the following:

- ◆ Important experiences that may be affecting your child
- ◆ Special medical needs
- ◆ Study habits at home
- ◆ TV habits
- ◆ After-school activities and special interests
- ◆ Feelings toward school

Again, welcome! Please feel free to contact me about your concerns.

Reprinted from TCM143 Form Letters and Assessment Comments, *Teacher Created Materials, 1992*

Introductory Letter to Parents #2

Dear Parents,

As the new school year begins I would like to introduce myself. My name is
_____. I have taught _____.

In addition to my education and teaching experience, I want you to know my philosophy of teaching children.

- ◆ I believe children deserve respect.
- ◆ I believe children should not be humiliated, hurt, or embarrassed.
- ◆ I believe a child's self-esteem should be nurtured tenderly.
- ◆ I believe my job is to teach until a child learns, rather than punish until he/she learns.
- ◆ I believe that if I am willing to say, "I'm sorry," when I make a mistake, I do not have to be afraid of making a mistake.
- ◆ I want your children to enjoy the learning process, and I want to help them develop their own motivation for learning. I hope to do my best to encourage your children to succeed in their attempts to learn.
- ◆ I believe modeling is the most powerful way to affect a child's learning. Please model the love of learning at home by reading to, and in front of, your child. In addition, set aside a quiet, well lit area with adequate space and supplies for your children to study. The study area should be in a place not far from the rest of the family.

Please feel free to contact me with concerns you may have this year. Our school number is _____. Please leave a message with _____, our school secretary, and I will return your call at my earliest convenience.

I am looking forward to an exciting and challenging year.

Reprinted from TCM143 Form Letters and Assessment Comments, *Teacher Created Materials, 1992*

Supplies for Home Study

Dear Parents,

Your help is needed in order for your child to have the best experience in completing homework. Students need to have something in which to carry their materials to and from school. A folder or backpack should be put in the same place at home each day. That way you will know where to look for any school notices or papers, and your child will know where to put homework when it is finished.

Help your child decide on the best time to do homework each day. Homework is an important extension of school work, and you can demonstrate its importance by scheduling a regular time for your child to complete it.

Having the proper equipment and supplies will make completing assignments easier, and you and your child will avoid frustration if you have the suggested items below.

- sharp pencils and/or pens
- crayons
- stapler
- tape
- construction paper
- glue and/or paste
- eraser
- marking pens
- ruler
- hole punch
- scissors
- notebook paper
- colored pencils

Set up a routine so that after homework is completed, your child puts it in the proper place. Help your child take responsibility; it is his/her homework, not yours.

Thank you for your help!

Reprinted from TCM143 Form Letters and Assessment Comments, *Teacher Created Materials, 1992*

Classroom Rules

Dear Parents,

We are off to a good start for the _____ school year. The children are all enthusiastic and eager to tackle _____ grade.

Our class motto is "Do your best." I am encouraging the children to put forth their best effort in everything they do.

To help ensure a successful school experience we have the following classroom rules:

Please review our class motto and these rules with your child to make sure that he/she understands them and how the rules will help us all to have a great year. Both you and your child should sign the statements on the tear-off portion below and return it to class.

Thanks for your support.

I have reviewed the class motto and rules with my child.

Parent's signature _____

I understand the class motto and rules and will try to follow them this year.

Child's signature _____

Reprinted from TCM143 Form Letters and Assessment Comments, *Teacher Created Materials, 1992*

Volunteer Help Needed

Dear Parents,

Children need to have good role models and warm, loving adults around to work with them. If you have a little extra time and the desire, your help will be greatly appreciated.

Please mark the options below that you will be willing to do at school.

☐ Read with students   ☐ Work in a computer lab

☐ Check student work   ☐ Work on an art project

☐ Work on cooking projects   ☐ Help with science projects

☐ Teach P.E. games   ☐ Help with music or dance

☐ Straighten centers   ☐ Help with a play

☐ Prepare teaching materials (photocopy, ditto, cut, etc.)

☐ Help students with work in another language. What do you speak in addition to English? _____

☐ Other (please specify) _____

I can use volunteers every day of the week. Circle those that are best for you and indicate a convenient time. I will notify you of any requirements for working in the classroom and when we will need you to start.

Monday   Tuesday   Wednesday   Thursday   Friday

_____   _____   _____   _____   _____

Thank you in advance for your help.

Reprinted from TCM143 Form Letters and Assessment Comments, *Teacher Created Materials, 1992*

Parent Letter for Homemade Rocks

Dear Parents,

We are studying rocks and minerals in our science class. Our next activity is to make rocks, for which each child will receive some play dough. They need to bring materials from home which can be mixed with the play dough to make a simulated rock. These items should be small, since the lump of play dough will be about the size of a golf ball. Items which would be good to use for this activity are as follows:

- small chips of rock, such as aquarium rocks
- synthetic jewels from old jewelry
- marbles
- small pebbles
- charcoal pieces
- scraps of aluminum foil

When the students are finished making their rocks, they will cut them open and compare them with real rocks which have been cut open. They will be able to keep their rocks at the end of our study.

Sincerely,

Reprinted from TCM636 Rocks and Minerals, *Teacher Created Materials, 1994*

Ways to Help Your Child

How can I help my child at home? That is the question most asked of teachers by interested parents. Here are some suggestions that may be of help to you:

- ☐ When booklets and papers are brought home, look at them; comment on them; go over them with your child. Show genuine interest in the work. This communicates the idea that education is important and encourages our children to do well in school.

- ☐ Talk with your children about school and everyday events.

- ☐ See that your child gets plenty of sleep. Encourage exercise and good nutrition.

- ☐ Monitor TV programs. TV can be instructional and also relaxing in proper doses at the proper time. Talk with them about the programs they watch. Turn off the TV to facilitate conversation.

- ☐ Encourage your child to do homework as early in the afternoon or evening as possible.

- ☐ Provide a quiet, well lit study area for your child. Set up a desk, table or area designated for study, not far from the other family members. Remember to provide materials such as pens, pencils, pencil sharpener, paper, dictionary, ruler, crayons, glue stick, and scissors.

- ☐ Take an active interest in your child's school work. Keep up with your child when he/she has a test and needs to study.

- ☐ Orally quiz a child to help him/her prepare for a test.

- ☐ If your child has trouble understanding something, try to help.

- ☐ Be aware of numerous study strategies, such as flash cards, that can be shared with your child.

- ☐ Read with your children. Encourage them to read for fun and discuss what they read.

*Reprinted from TCM*143 Form Letters and Assessment Comments, *Teacher Created Materials,* *1992*

Dear Parents,

This month we will begin a unit on apples. Please have your child bring one apple to school on Friday.

Thank You,
Mrs. Jones

Reprinted from TCM123 Fall Time Savers, *Teacher Created Materials, 1989*

Stepping Stone School
PRINCIPAL'S PEN

[graphic colored
by the child]

To: (Name)
(Address) [data filled out by the child]
(Date)

Dear Parents,

Carnival News: Site council parents and the Stepping Stone School Student Council put together a super Halloween Carnival. There were fifteen booths in all and many Stepping Stone children came out to enjoy our games. Thanks to all for making this a successful activity. Special thanks to Angela Adams for the extra time and work she gave to the carnival. Without her, I am certain we wouldn't have gotten the idea off the ground. Thanks, Angela!!

Home-School Partnership: November will be an exciting month at SSS. Our partnership schools will join us on November 15 for tours and meetings. Teachers, parents, and students from our county region will visit Stepping Stone. Together we will discuss ideas for funding office equipment for the Parent Center and developing a Partnership-sponsored career day for students.

Report Cards: The first trimester will end on November 20. Report cards will be available for parents to pick up at our report card day beginning at 2 P. M. and ending at 8 P. M. At that time parents can each have fifteen minute conferences with teachers. Parents can expect to receive a printed report card and a discipline report. Parents who are unable to attend the report card day conference will receive the report card in the mail. They are asked to sign and return a statement of receipt.

Continued on the next page

PRINCIPAL'S PEN *(cont.)*

Elective Program: Students who have maintained grades of "C" or better in all subjects will be eligible to choose a new elective for the second trimester. The electives include astronomy, ecology, computer science, Spanish, geography, world literature, and art. Students who did not maintain the "C" minimum will be assigned for one hour a day to the individual instruction lab for one-on-one instruction by a trained tutor.

Partnership Meeting: The next regularly scheduled SSS Partnership meeting is November 21 at 5:30 P. M. in the Parent Center. All parents are encouraged to attend. We will be discussing the library budget and the upcoming School Site Review. Please call the school office or Parent Center if you have any questions.

General News: Remember last year our SSS **academic pentathlon** team won the county championship. We are pleased to announce that again this year the team will be coached by Mr. Stackpole and Ms. Newsome. Team members are currently being recruited, and study materials for the academic competition have been ordered and received. Your child will receive information about the pentathlon and should be bringing it home to you within the week. Be on the lookout!

Two of our teachers have been asked to make a presentation at the **Multiple Intelligences Conference** in Kentucky next month. Mr. Ford and Ms. Taurus were selected from a pool of 100 applicants. We are pleased and honored to have them on our staff and wish them well with their presentation.

Many of us who spend time with children, whether as parents, teachers, or administrators, want to know **what we can do to help improve their self-esteem**. We know that improved self-esteem leads to happier children who are better learners. Thanks to some literature research by our Partnership team, we want to provide you with some secrets:

1. Spend quality time each day with your children. This is an opportunity to hear what they did and what is on their minds.

2. Make positive statements to your children as often as possible. No one has enough armor to withstand a constant barrage of "no" and "don't."

Continued on the next page

3. When disagreements occur, argue only about inaccurate facts or statements. Remember, everyone has opinions. Sometimes we must agree to disagree.

4. Reach out and touch. Everyone wants it. A touch will communicate more than words.

5. Smile. Be happy around your children.

6. Allow children to develop responsibility by having responsibility for some household chore.

7. Be honest with your children. Children will undoubtedly learn their response patterns from parents. Honesty also shows children you trust them.

8. Separate the behavior from the individual. In problem situations make certain the child knows the behavior, not the child, is unacceptable.

9. Deal with the here-and-now issues. Dredging up the past will block communication within the family.

10. Work on your own positive self-esteem. Happy, well-adjusted human beings who genuinely care for others make excellent parents.

Upcoming events:

(list dates, events, contact person, and phone number)

Have a good month!

Sincerely,

Penelope Principal

Preconference Letter

Dear Parents of _____,

Our parent conference is scheduled for _____. I am looking forward to meeting with you to discuss your child's progress. In order for us to plan this conference, it is important that you express your feelings, interests, and areas of concern.

Please respond to the following items and return the bottom portion to me by _____. Your help is appreciated.

Check one:

    _____ This conference time is fine.

    _____ I am unable to attend at the time scheduled. Please call me at _____ between the hours of _____ and _____ to reschedule.

What is your child's attitude toward school? _____

What are his/her interests and activities outside school? _____

Is there anything else you might tell me about your child which will help me to know him/her better?

Please write any comments on the back of this letter.

Suggested Topics for Conference

- homework
- health
- curriculum

- self-control
- friends
- self-confidence

- listening skills
- respect for authority
- other

Please circle three topics from the above areas to discuss during our conference.

Reprinted from TCM143 Form Letters and Assessment Comments, *Teacher Created Materials, 1992*

Stepping Stone School
Family Science Night
Friday, April 10th
Group Challenges

Come join us for the annual Family Science Night Group Challenge! This year we will begin our program at 4 P. M. with family teams making kites and having a kite flying contest. The kite flying contest will be in the field east of the multipurpose room.

At 6 P. M. we will have a potluck supper in the multipurpose room. Bring one dish and place settings for every three people.

Then at 7 P. M. the GROUP CHALLENGES will begin! You may have up to three (3) people on your team, including parents, grandparents, older sisters and brothers, or any other relative or friend.

To participate in the GROUP CHALLENGES, please fill out the entry form below. Please print or type. Fill in all the lines. Return your entry blank to your teacher or the Parent Center no later than April 2.

****

Group Challenges Entry Form

Team Name: _____

Team Members (list all 3): _____

Grade of student: _____   Teacher: _____

Check the event in which your team will participate:

_____ Dome on the Range	_____ Barge Building	
_____ Rubber Nest	_____ Lofty Loopers	
_____ Pasta Proboscis	_____ Airborne	

In Conclusion

Where Have We Been, Where Are We Going?

In the beginning of this book you were asked to visualize a school, your school, where:

- ◆ the children are excited about learning

- ◆ discipline problems are minimal

- ◆ the learning environment is structured so all children have an excellent opportunity to succeed

- ◆ students work on meaningful curriculum projects that extend beyond the school day to evenings and weekends where their parents work with them to succeed

- ◆ the parents support the school politically and with resources

- ◆ parents and community members provide tutoring to students in need

- ◆ parents bring their career, cultural, linguistic, and other skills to school to enrich the curriculum

> In the beginning of this book you were asked to visualize a school, your school, where the children are excited about learning.

Certainly, building a partnership between home and school will make children more excited about learning as their parents become more involved in helping the children at home and become more active at the school.

Discipline problems are reduced when the parents are working with the schools.

The learning environment is more exciting for children when the teachers have talked to the parents and have insights into the children. Through the family night activities and other suggestions, students can work on meaningful projects that extend beyond the school day and work with their parents.

Public opinion surveys consistently indicate that the more people know about their school, the higher they rate it. Building partnerships will increase that knowledge, which certainly can lead to increased parental political and resource support for the school.

In a partnership school, parents and community members are invited to provide tutoring as needed, both in the classroom and at the Parent Center.

Parents, as partners with the school, bring their career, linguistic, and other skills to the school to enrich the curriculum and make the school an exciting place to be.

If we work together to build communication partnerships between the schools and the parents, we all win. In working together we grow a child who is more successful academically, who understands the value of working partnerships, and who has a sense of belonging and of being loved. If we can extend that sense of partnership more broadly into our society, we can make the Earth better for the children and the children better for the Earth.

References

Aronson, M. (1994). <u>Teaching individuals</u>. Manuscript submitted for publication.

California State Department of Education. (1987). <u>Caught in the middle: Educational reform for young adolescents in California public schools</u>. Sacramento, CA: Author.

Carnegie Council on Adolescent Development. (1989). <u>Turning points: Preparing American youth for the 21st century</u>. New York: Carnegie Corporation of New York.

Covey, S. R. (1989). <u>The 7 habits of highly effective people</u>. New York: Simon and Schuster.

Elam, S. M., Rose, L. C., & Gallup, A. M. (1992). <u>The 24th annual Gallup/Phi Delta Kappa poll of the public's attitudes toward the public schools</u>. Guilford, CT: Dushkin Publishing Group.

Elam, S. M., Rose, L. C., & Gallup, A. M. (1994). The 26th Annual Gallup/Phi Delta Kappa poll of the public's attitudes toward the public schools. <u>Phi Delta Kappan, 76</u>(1), 41–56.

Finney, P. (1993, May 17). The PTA/Newsweek national education survey. <u>Newsweek, 121</u>(20), S10-S12.

Gilman, R. (Ed.). (Winter, 1991). <u>In context: A quarterly of humane sustainable culture</u>. Bainbridge Island, WA: Context Institute.

Goodlad, J. I. (1984). <u>A place called school: Prospects for the future</u>. New York: McGraw Hill.

Greenwald, J. (1994, November 14). The new service class. <u>Time</u>, 72–74.

Holtgate, S. (1994). <u>Marriage patterns in Khumer youth</u>. Unpublished master's thesis, California State University, Stanislaus.

Lee, V. E., & Croninger, R. G. (1994). The relative importance of home and school in the development of literacy skills for middle-grade students. <u>American Journal of Education, 102</u>, 286–329.

Mullis, I. V. S., Campbell, J. R., & Farstrup, A. E. (1993). <u>NAEP 1992 reading report card for the nation and states</u>. Washington, D. C.: National Center for Education Statistics.

National Commission on Children. (1991). <u>Speaking of kids: A national survey of children and parents</u>. Washington, D.C.: Author.

Peter, L. J. (1977). <u>Peter's quotations: Ideas for our time</u>. New York: William Morrow.

Rich, D. (1987). <u>Teachers and parents: An adult-to-adult approach</u>. Washington, D.C.: National Education Association Professional Library.

Stevenson, C. (1992). <u>Teaching ten to fourteen year olds</u>. New York: Longman.

Swap, S. M. (1993). <u>Developing home-school partnerships: From concepts to practices</u>. New York: Teachers College Press.

U. S. Bureau of the Census. (1994). <u>Educational attainment in the United States: March, 1993 and 1992</u>. (Current Population Reports No. P20-476). Washington, D. C.: Author.

U. S. Department of Education. (1994). <u>Strong families, strong schools: Building community partnerships for learning</u>. Washington, D. C.: Author.

References *(cont.)*

Teacher Created Materials
Reference List

TCM #143 Form Letters and Assessment Comments for your Whole Language Classroom
TCM #149 Year-Round Teacher Tips
TCM #636 Rocks and Minerals
TCM #123 Fall Time Savers

Other Suggested Materials

TCM #144 How to Manage Your Whole Language Classroom
TCM #504 Portfolios and Other Assessments

TCM #506 Middle School Assessment

TCM #770 Math Assessment Grades 1–2
TCM #774 Math Assessment Grades 3–4
TCM #778 Math Assessment Grades 5–6
TCM #771 Science Assessment Grades 1–2
TCM #775 Science Assessment Grades 3–4
TCM #779 Science Assessment Grades 5–6
TCM #772 Social Studies Assessment Grades 1–2
TCM #776 Social Studies Assessment Grades 3–4
TCM #780 Social Studies Assessment Grades 5–6
TCM #773 Language Arts Assessment Grades 1–2
TCM #777 Language Arts Assessment Grades 3–4
TCM #781 Language Arts Assessment Grades 5–6

TCM #124 Winter Time Savers
TCM #125 Spring Time Savers

TCM #148 Year-Round Time Savers